CUB REPORTERS

CUB REPORTERS

American Children's Literature and
Journalism in the Golden Age

Paige Gray

Cover image: Jack Delano, *Newsboy selling the Chicago Defender*, April 1924. Library of Congress Prints and Photographs Division. https://www.loc.gov/item/2017872943

Published by State University of New York Press, Albany

© 2019 State University of New York

All rights reserved

Printed in the United States of America

No part of this book may be used or reproduced in any manner whatsoever without written permission. No part of this book may be stored in a retrieval system or transmitted in any form or by any means including electronic, electrostatic, magnetic tape, mechanical, photocopying, recording, or otherwise without the prior permission in writing of the publisher.

For information, contact State University of New York Press, Albany, NY
www.sunypress.edu

Library of Congress Cataloging-in-Publication Data

Names: Gray, Paige, author.
Title: Cub reporters : American children's literature and journalism in the Golden Age / Paige Gray.
Description: Albany, NY : State University of New York Press, [2019] | Includes bibliographical references.
Identifiers: LCCN 2018040414 | ISBN 9781438475394 (hardcover) | ISBN 9781438475417 (e-book) | ISBN 9781438475400 (paperback)
Subjects: LCSH: Children's stories, American—History and criticism. | Young adult fiction, American—History and criticism. | Journalism and literature—United States—History—20th century. | Reporters and reporting in literature. | Reporters and reporting—United States.
Classification: LCC PS374.C454 G73 2019 | DDC 810.9/928209034—dc23
LC record available at https://lccn.loc.gov/2018040414

10 9 8 7 6 5 4 3 2 1

To my amazing, supportive family and my adopted family of friends, which includes so many—from kindred spirits I've known since childhood to those wonderful people I've met in newsrooms, classrooms, libraries, and college campuses over the years. You help me stay curious and creative.

CONTENTS

Illustrations / ix

Acknowledgments / xi

Introduction American Children's Literature, the "Yellow-Kid Reporter" Era, and Artifice / xiii

Chapter 1 Carrying the Banner: Horatio Alger, Jr., the Newsboy, and the Paper / 1

Chapter 2 Making News and Faking Truth: Richard Harding Davis, the Reporter, and American Youth / 17

Chapter 3 A Spectacle of Girls: L. Frank Baum, Women Reporters, and the Man Behind the Curtain in Early Twentieth-Century America / 41

Chapter 4 Join the Club: African American Children's Literature, Social Change, and the Chicago Defender Junior / 69

Conclusion "I Want to Know Everything": Harriet the Spy and New Journalism / 89

Notes / 103

Works Cited / 115

Index / 129

ILLUSTRATIONS

Figure I.1. The opening of the Hogan's Alley roof garden. / xxv

Figure 1.1. Mattie rehearsing "Carrying the Banner" from Newsies. / 2

Figure 1.2. Ragged Dick series. / 4

Figure 2.1. Undated photograph of Richard Harding Davis. / 19

Figure 3.1. Nellie Bly. / 42

Figure 3.2. Dorothy misses the hot-air balloon. / 43

Figure 3.3. *Aunt Jane's Nieces on Vacation* cover artwork. / 45

Figure 3.4. Round the World with Nellie Bly. / 49

Figure 4.1. Banner for the Chicago Defender Junior. / 73

Figure 4.2. Bud Billiken Club membership form. / 77

ix

ACKNOWLEDGMENTS

I would like to sincerely thank my friend and mentor Eric Tribunella for his guidance and insight during the many stages of this project since its genesis during my first days as a graduate student at the University of Southern Mississippi. I am also indebted to Luis Iglesias, Jonathan Barron, and Alexandra Valint for their support and invaluable contributions to this project. My interest in pursuing children's literature as a focus of inquiry began while working on my undergraduate honors thesis at Indiana University. The feminist possibilities of L. Frank Baum's texts were illuminated for me thanks to my wonderful thesis advisor, Ellen MacKay. But my specific intervention into the critical conversation came after working with the journalism faculty at Columbia College Chicago—Suzanne McBride, Norma Green, Len Strazewski, and Curtis Lawrence. I also would like to thank members of the Children's Literature Association. The annual conference of this organization gave me an early audience and constructive feedback for much of this project's initial research. I could not have developed the ideas presented in *Cub Reporters* without the access and assistance provided by multiple archival collections. Specifically, I would like to thank Ellen Ruffin and the staff at the de Grummond Children's Literature Collection of the University of Southern Mississippi, Hoke Perkins and the staff at the Albert and Shirley Small Special Collections Library at the University of Virginia, and the Archives and Manuscripts staff at the New York Public Library. Additionally, thank you to the Johns Hopkins University Press and the Children's Literature Association for allowing me to publish an extended version of "Join the Club," which first appeared in the *Children's Literature Association Quarterly* 42.2, as well as Lexington Books, who published an earlier version of "Spectacle of Girls" in *Girls' Series Fiction and American Popular Culture* (2016) and permitted me to reproduce it here.

INTRODUCTION

American Children's Literature, the "Yellow-Kid Reporter" Era, and Artifice

Pretend it's 1896. You live in New York City. It's Sunday.

That means today is the day for the supplement edition of *The World* newspaper, and *that* means *Hogan's Alley* and the Yellow Kid. In the days when the printed newspaper defined the world for the reading public, Joseph Pulitzer's *World* attempted to report and reimagine it in bold, innovative ways, including through the use of color and comics. *Hogan's Alley*, a one-panel illustration starring the uncouth Yellow Kid and his gang of street children, became one of the pioneers of this daring, fledgling form that had discovered a new way to—well, what exactly *did* it do? The introduction of bright visual hues and irreverent characters made it a novelty feature and popular amusement. But it also functioned as biting political satire and cultural commentary, and it did so through the figures of children. Whether young or old, it's not unlikely that you would have eagerly sought out a copy of *The World* on Sundays. But what "news" of the world would you have absorbed? What was the Yellow Kid reporting to his readers?

If you had picked up the Sunday *World* on July 26, 1896, you may have skipped straight to the supplement to see the new raucous *Hogan's Alley*. It might not have been giving its audience new information about the latest happenings in New York or Washington, but in some fashion, it was usually saying something *about* those happenings. And something about American childhood. And something about storytelling. And something about race, gender, and class in an America that was growing more urban. But you probably wouldn't have thought about that. You would have been more interested in the fact that *The World* was now publishing this strange, funny drawing every Sunday—in color.

That was news. Turning to the July 26, 1896, installment of *Hogan's Alley*, you would have been dazzled by the tints and tones of the elaborate scene, which, in this particular edition, appears to take place at a theater. And you possibly would have chuckled at the thought of street kids taking on dramatic performance. Now that would be something, wouldn't it? But what about the actual news of that particular Sunday? What was the distinction between the news of *The World* proper and the "news" of *Hogan's Alley*?

During the summer of 1896, American journalists kept themselves busy—and entertained—chronicling the latest developments of the upcoming presidential election. The front page of the Sunday, July 26, edition of *The World* announced recent events arising out of the Populist Party Convention in St. Louis. The predominant headline indicates that presumptive candidate William Jennings Bryan "Is in Doubt" and that "His Acceptance of the Populist Nomination for President Depends 'Entirely Upon the Conditions Attached'" (New York *World* 1). But the political theater and the growing complexity of the American party system evidenced on *The World*'s front page had to compete against other embellished renderings of daily life, including headlines detailing "ONE BURGLAR FLOORED. Young Mr. Minnot Grappled With a Cracksman and Captured Him" and "RESCUED TWO GIRLS. They Were Locked Into a Factory Building and Screamed" (New York *World* 1). The most sensational story, that of a physician's rapid mental collapse once he believes his wife dead, sits under a multideck headline that introduces new titillating information with each sentence, spaced out to force readers further into the article while simultaneously providing just enough of the story to satisfy a superficial news perusal:

> GRIEF TURNED HIS BRAIN.
>
> Thinking He Had Killed His Wife, Dr. Maximilian M. Weil Attempted Suicide.
>
> DRANK CARBOLIC ACID FIRST.
>
> But the Poison Did Not Act Quickly,
>
> So He Gashed His Throat with a Razor.
>
> HIS YOUNG WIFE HAD ONLY FAINTED.
>
> He Had Given Her Morphine for Hysteria—Strong Constitution May Enable Him to Recover. (New York *World* 1)

Each subsequent line functions as a new scene that heightens the drama of this *Romeo and Juliet*–like incident, exquisitely crafted to entice readers away from the other Sunday-edition competition in the crowded New York newspaper market. Certainly, the stage for this extraordinary domestic drama, as well as that of the grand spectacle of American political theater, is the newspaper, the "public institution and a public teacher," according to *The World's* publisher, Joseph Pulitzer (657).

Indeed, the newspaper—journalism—succeeds and sells using the art of artifice. But this is not another condemnation of "fake news," the popular epithet so favored by President Donald Trump to discredit mainstream-media reporting in the wake of his surprise 2016 electoral victory. And, of course, journalism depends on the principles of verification, transparency, and accuracy. But that is not the focus here. No, *Cub Reporters* seeks to embrace and reclaim artifice by looking at some of its greatest champions—children. More specifically, children as rendered in children's literature, but this book also considers flesh-and-blood children, those young people who inspired and were inspired by the Golden Age of American children's literature during the late nineteenth and early twentieth centuries. The years between the Civil War and World War I also approximate a "golden age" of the newspaper, a time when "the American newspaper rapidly became a cultural institution of undeniable force" and is eventually "universally accepted as one of the foundation stones of American social life" (Douglas 7, vi). Yet, returning to the front page of *The World*, with those shrewdly crafted headlines and narrative revisions of political and domestic life, it evidences the *artifice* of the newspaper; it is a constructed form requiring skill, thought, and purpose. Of course, this is no secret, but the artistry of the news can be easy to overlook when presented and packaged as natural fact. *Cub Reporters* explores the relationship between young people and the hegemony of the newspaper as depicted in children's literature and other texts of the era, and it considers how children destabilize ideological narratives of truth, news, and fact—predominantly in the literary world, but sometimes in the actual world.

My critical methodology relies on historicism to illustrate the influential exchange between American culture and its texts—literary, journalistic, and ephemeral forms of communication. In this model, the literary, political, social, and economic components of culture exist together in a web, and thus the events occurring in one area affect the entire web. As such, the fundamental structure of my study draws from Stephen Greenblatt's New Historicism tenets: "The notion of culture as a text" with "[m]ajor works of art remain[ing] centrally important" (Gallagher and Greenblatt 9), or what Louis Montrose has called the "historicity of texts, the textuality of history" (8). Michael McKeon describes "the basic tool of historical method" as being "the strategic dialectic between the division and the conflation of categories" (49). Categories, here, can refer not only to academic disciplines, but to varied textual artifacts. In historicist approaches to literary studies, this means considering not only texts outside the canon, but outside of traditional literature—newspaper articles and advertisements, printed ephemera, photographs, and images—in order to destabilize the hegemonic cultural narrative. Variety and difference allow for a "dialectic of opposition," which McKeon calls "a tool of discovery, a way of opening up possibilities for the interpretation of historical phenomena" (49). *Cub Reporters* employs such an approach in an attempt to "ope[n] up" these "possibilities" found in works of children's literature that address the creative processes of narrativizing, making meaning, and selling reality through the venue of the newspaper, processes I collectively call *artifice*.

Regardless of their categorization under what Hayden White characterizes as "real events" or "imaginary events" (23), the discourses found in literature, history, and journalism seek to tell stories—they narrativize. Historical or literary narrative "might well be considered a solution to a problem of general human concern," offers White. This problem, he states, is one of "how to translate *knowing* into *telling*" and "fashioning human experience into a form assimilable to structures of meaning that are generally human rather than culture-specific" (1). Roland Barthes explains that it is simply human to do this; it is how we utilize knowledge to make sense of the world, because narrative "ceaselessly substitutes meaning for the straightforward copy of the events recounted" (119). "Narrative," Barthes explains, "does not show, does not imitate," but reveals "meaning, that of a higher order of relation which also has its emotions, its hopes, its dangers, its triumphs" (124). There is an expectation that fictions of "imaginary events" should do this, but White posits that we want the same of our accounts of reality. He thinks the "value attached to narrativity in the representation of real events arises out of a desire to have real events display the coherence, integrity, fullness, and closure of an image of life that is and can only be imaginary" (23).

Communication theorist James W. Carey depicts the juncture between narrative and the "real events" of journalism in rather eloquent terms, writing that in studying the history of the profession, scholars can "grasp the form of consciousness, the imaginations, the interpretations of reality [that] journalism has contained" (27). He views journalism history as "the story of growth and transformation of the human mind as formed and expressed by one of the most significant forms in which the mind has conceived and expressed itself during the last three hundred years—the journalistic report" (27). Similarly, communication scholar Barbie Zelizer describes journalism's narrative tendency as an asset because of its ability to resonate with and matter to readers. "Journalism as narrative is another way to account for journalism's commonality," Zelizer writes (26). Additionally, journalistic narrative "helps us construct our view of the world, by allowing us to share stories within culturally and socially explicit codes of meaning" (26).

Essential to giving power over to these journalistic "codes of meaning" is the understanding or awareness of the constructive process that Zelizer discusses, and the same rings true with children's literature, which has provided "codes of meaning" for American culture. American children's literature has shaped ideals and standards for what childhood "should be," ideals and standards that have generally emanated from middle- or upper-class white cultural backgrounds and ideologies. In her crucial contribution to the field of children's literature, *Kiddie Lit: The Cultural Construction of Children's Literature in America*, Beverly Lyon Clark says, "[W]e tend to assume that what it means to be a child, what it means for an adult to understand a child—never mind what it means to write from or for a child's perspective—is unproblematic" (9). This "unproblematic," uncritical means of digesting human experience—a means often applied to popular, widespread culture such as journalism and children's literature and media—not only flattens its complexity and richness, it risks oppression and dehumanization. However, exploring the process and product of the ways in which "codes of meaning" come to fruition invites readers to engage. Kim Reynolds writes that children's literature has the potential to "expose, critique, and adjust the schemata by which we interpret the world" and can "sow and nurture the seeds of social change" (5). How might American children's literature have sown these seeds during the golden age? And what are the implications of the newspaper's presence in the genre at this time? Turning to Michel Foucault and his work on resisting discourses of power, how are readers asked to begin "looking at things otherwise" (328)?

Artifice and the Golden Age

Because of significant social, cultural, and technological changes after the Civil War, American children's literature proliferated in the late nineteenth century and introduced more narratives that explored imaginative pursuits instead of (or in addition to) emphatic moral or didactic objectives. Education reform and advances in printing allowed for innovative publishing possibilities aimed at a larger audience of young readers. During this period, "the ability to reproduce photographs" and "the mass production of color images ... led to lavishly produced and illustrated books for children [that] ... helped make best-selling authors of Robert Louis Stevenson, Rudyard Kipling, Mark Twain, Frances

Hodgson Burnett, E. Nesbit, Beatrix Potter, Louisa May Alcott, and A. A. Milne" (Zipes et al. xxviii–xxix). Children's literature as a genre influenced more than children, as all ages read books now considered children's classics. Novels such as Twain's *The Adventures of Tom Sawyer* (1876) "appealed to both children and adults and were reviewed by leading literary critics in magazines with wide circulation" (Zipes et al. xxviii–xxix). Young people also entertained themselves with "sensationalized fiction offered by the stories of 'Oliver Optic' and dime novels, the latter of which were filled with the exploits of western heroes, and (from the 1880s) with stories about detectives" (Carpenter and Prichard 553). In other words, American children's literature became more ambitious in scope and theme in addition to reaching a wide audience of assorted readers, and in doing so, helped fashion American culture's ideas about children and childhood—not unlike the ways the newspaper helped shape the public's ideas of the country and world.

Postbellum children's literature also offered a cultural space for writers to engage with and respond to the journalism industry and its means of reporting (and selling) news, or fact. Yet given the newspapers' growing use of new storytelling methods through sensationalized writing, stunt reporting, and even comics such as *Hogan's Alley*, the challenge of what I call *artifice* arises. How can the newspaper or journalism industry tell truth when it is inherently a creative endeavor? This is an old question on which much has been written, and I'm not attempting to answer it. Instead, I'm interested in exploring how writers of the time grappled with this question through children's literature. *Cub Reporters* contends that in American children's literature of the golden age, children function as reporters of artifice. The genre responds to the rise of the newspaper by challenging the authority of news through the actions of young people; it acknowledges journalism's consequential influence but critiques its power in the newspaper-centric works that I consider. Ultimately, through the newspaper worlds depicted in the works discussed in *Cub Reporters*, children reveal the overriding truth of *artifice*—and they relish it. If the newspaper—which structures the general public's understanding of the nation—is shown as crafted, then *all* is artifice, and thus young people have the power to recreate "truth," particularly in terms of how culture understands the constructs of childhood and youth.

Cub Reporters shows children's literature of the Golden Age subverting the idea of news; journalism, in these works, is not a reporting of fact, but a reporting of artifice—cub reporters report the truth of artifice. In general, I use "report" and "reporter" in a broad sense. Some examples have child characters literally engaging in journalistic behavior, and in other instances, the text works as a symbolic "reporter" by showing the process of artifice. I demonstrate this idea by analyzing works of children's literature from this period that specifically address newspapers or the journalism industry in order to contextualize the relationship and influence between children's culture (or, more inclusively, youth culture) and journalism. The texts discussed signal an embrace of artifice as a means to access individual agency. This is significant because such a move encourages child (and adult) readers to deconstruct and create the world anew for themselves—to find agency through artifice.

Artifice, as I employ the term in *Cub Reporters*, broadly refers to human-made apparatus—artistic, technological, psychological, cultural, or otherwise—devised and used to both communicate ideas and compel others to acknowledge those ideas. It can refer to works of individual invention or the production of larger social constructs: gender, race, class, childhood, adulthood. Generally speaking, artifice exists in contrast to the natural, biological world and showcases the human power of creativity. That is a lot of work for one word, but by allowing *artifice* to serve as an umbrella term for human creativity in all its senses, I hope to erase the adverse implications of the word that associate it with mendacity and malicious intent. Instead, I aim to use the term's wide reach to reinforce individual agency. Throughout the book, I focus on more "local" manifestations of artifice—artistic and creative choices or actions by writers, characters, reporters—to show how larger concepts that are often deemed "natural" or "absolute" also reflect artifice, and are therefore available for revision. As such, *Cub Reporters* investigates how depictions of young people in late nineteenth- and early twentieth-century America use artifice to dismantle preexisting narratives.

The *Oxford English Dictionary* provides one definition of *artifice* as "[h]uman skill or workmanship as opposed to nature or a natural phenomenon," and similarly, "[t]echnical skill; artistry, ingenuity" ("artifice"). Artifice is that which we *purposefully* create and which requires or displays a level of imagination, curiosity, or originality. It showcases the very human capacity *to create*, and thus the word *artifice* often conflates the skill and that which the skill produces. But thinking of art in the classical sense as that which mimics nature, successful artifice should, according to this line of reasoning, obscure artificiality. In that sense, the *OED* gives definitions of *artifice* that refer to "[s]kill in devising and using expedients; artfulness, cunning, trickery" and "an ingenious expedient, a clever stratagem; (chiefly in negative sense) a manoeuvre or device intended to deceive, a trick" ("artifice"). Here, I am interested in exploring how and when artifice is acknowledged—when its craftsmanship is ignored, when it is embraced, and the consequences of this exposure and concealment in regard to American children's literature and journalism. In looking at the two together, we see how artifice can be reclaimed and reconfigured. Rather than hold merely negative connotations because of its associations with deception, artifice can serve as a form of liberation. When embraced, artifice functions as a call to arms, to action. It reminds us that we write and create and craft the news around us, and that we can have the power, if not the responsibility, to change the headlines.

However, I do want to underscore the double-edged sword of artifice, particularly given this cultural moment and the democratization of news through social media. When I allude to "changing the headlines," I use the phrase to connect artifice and action, writing and being. And while I use this connection to promote ideas of human understanding, acceptance, and equality, artifice can indeed be used in ways that obscure, erode, or ignore widely accepted truths in order to tyrannize and persecute. Artifice always exists in a nexus of power, and it is a tool of power. There's a popular quotation generally attributed to Pablo Picasso—"Anything you can imagine is real." This is both exhilarating and terrifying.

Susan Sontag's famous articulation of camp undoubtedly influenced my conception of artifice. In "Notes on 'Camp'" (1964), Sontag proposes that camp is "[a] sensibility (as distinct from an idea)," and for Sontag, "the essence of Camp is its love of the unnatural: of artifice and exaggeration" (259). More than an artistic mode or "sensibility," I'm concerned with the "idea" of artifice from which camp stems. Artifice itself doesn't exhibit a "love" for the "unnatural." Rather, it provokes examination of what constitutes naturalness.

Using the term *artifice* addresses and links together the inherent contradictions found in children's literature and journalism. In each, the act of creation defies, or at least somewhat complicates, its mission; adults establish the world of children's literature, and in journalism, curated stories attempt to accurately mirror reality. In regard to children's literature, David Rudd aptly states that "the child is necessarily both constructed and constructive, and this hybrid border country is worthy of exploration" (25). That is, the idea of childhood comes from adult imaginings primarily delivered through the vehicle of children's literature, and these imaginings inevitably alter, edit, or enhance actual childhood experiences. "Constructing literary childhood, adults often replay the patterns of their own early lives," writes Anne Scott McLeod, "sometimes romanticizing, sometimes justifying them, sometimes bringing them to a more satisfying conclusion than they achieved in reality" (13). In this process, literary childhood shapes ideas of "reality," the ideas of what childhood is for readers and the culture at large. But as Rudd posits, the child is also "constructive," and a process of redefinition can take place in a "hybrid border country," that psyche-space of give-and-take where the reciprocal processes of creation and reception occur. This practice of invention constitutes artifice, and as such, reality requires artifice—or, as the "cub reporters" throughout this book evidence, reality is a reworkable piece of artifice.

Artifice, as I see it, conflates notions of the vague conceit of the non-"natural" with the notions of human-produced creativity and reinvention to force reconsideration of preexisting truths. In nineteenth-century America, active experimentation with and interest in artifice manifests throughout literature and journalism, with writers questioning the boundaries between fact and fiction, creation and deception. In his exhaustive *Bunk* (2017), Kevin Young argues that during this time, America was preoccupied with (and is still preoccupied with) what he collectively calls "bunk," or "hoaxes, humbug, plagiarists, phonies, post-facts, and fake news," which certainly could be considered extensions of artifice, particularly artifice as understood in the traditional sense of counterfeiting and duplicity. "Nineteenth-century America regularly reveled in the contradictions of what famed showman P. T. Barnum called *humbug*, his many audiences taking pleasure in hoaxing and being hoaxed," Young says, subtly hinting at the historical similarities between that moment in time and our own present one (7). Young sees "humbug" or "hoaxes" as a means for the country "to marvel at its mysteries, question its hypocrisies, and express contradictions of freedom and slavery, exploration and faith," and asserts that American literary paragons Edgar Allan Poe and Mark Twain "questioned truth rather than questing after it" (11). Indeed, Mark Canada finds that nineteenth-century American writers questioned truth through exploring the power and reach of the newspaper, noting that while many authors of this period also worked or started in journalism, "even more wrote *about* journalism" (5). Canada looks at how "American writers respond[ed] to the *phenomenon* of journalism, develop[ed] their own sense of truth-telling in opposition to journalism's example, and craft[ed] their own 'news' about the world" (5). Extending from and synthesizing certain elements of these projects, I claim that examples of Golden Age children's literature use the newspaper to promote artifice as a means to upset unquestioned power narratives and expose the instability of "truth" and that which is deemed "natural" by society. Truth and nature, according to the texts I consider, rest in the human capacity to create.

The Yellow Kid

Looking at artifice's interplay between children's literature and journalism at the turn of the last century illuminates how we think about not only children's literature and journalism, but also American childhood, national identity, creative and intellectual pursuits, and the power dynamics implicated in the policing of knowledge. The figure of the child has reliably been "seized on as a vehicle for nostalgia or as a symbol of the future's promise" dating back to the earliest days of the young republic (Griswold 24). As Jerry Griswold notes, "[F]rom the beginning of American history through the nineteenth century, Americans consistently saw their political history in terms of the development of a child," thus rendering the child and children's literature important political tools (13). When it exposes and engages with artifice, whether intentionally or unavoidably, American children's literature celebrates the potential of the child reader (and the adult reader) to be an artificer—that is, a producer and critical thinker as opposed to a passive, subjugated consumer.

By means of political theater and sensationalized drama, *The World*'s front page on July 26, 1896, effectively employs artifice to report current affairs and sell newspapers. But the publication focuses on the reporting of these current affairs; its focus is generally not the artifice itself. Flipping to the *Hogan's Alley* panel, the child characters focus on the artifice. They bring the news of artifice through questioning the boundaries of not only theater, but also childhood. This newspaper comic and its central figure, the Yellow Kid, distill the relationship between journalism and children's literature during this period. *Hogan's Alley*, at the intersection of journalism and children's literature, underscores the artifice of its surrounding newspaper pages by reveling in the strangeness and process of its own construct.

By the late nineteenth century, the American newspaper had become a well-established cultural and social institution, incorporating artifice seamlessly, albeit, at times, sensationally. A census report from 1902 states that in 1900, the number of published daily newspaper titles in the fifty largest American cities totaled 451 (Rossiter 17). Between 1890 and 1900 alone, the number of daily morning and afternoon newspapers in major cities increased by nearly 60 percent (Rossiter 17). According to David W. Sachsman, the newspaper of early America shifted the focus of its coverage over the course of the nineteenth century, gradually concerning itself more with "crime and corruption, filth and freaks, and gore and guts," with some publications including "sensationalized coverage [that] was fabrication" (xxii). In regard to the eventual development of the yellow journalism, W. Joseph Campbell maintains that even though

American history castigates it, much of today's journalism remains indebted to its industry advancements, such as "distinctive ... typography," "lavish use of illustrations," and "aggressive newsgathering techniques" (2). "For all its flaws and virtues," Campbell writes, "yellow journalism exerted a powerful influence in American journalism at the turn of the twentieth century" (2). He asserts that today's news media could be thought of as "'reformed' yellow journalism" (2).

The innovative, bold maneuvers of the late-nineteenth-century press introduced a variety of stunts and features in the attempt to attract and build readership, one of these novelties being the comic panel and comic strip. Of *Hogan's Alley*'s "Yellow Kid," Mike Benton says he "proved to be such a circulation booster for the newspaper that the future of the comic strip was assured" (14). The outrageously popular comic created by Richard Outcault consisted of one large panel and featured a group of tenement children—including Mickey Dugan, the "Yellow Kid." The character typifies an impoverished street waif through his bald head, presumably shaved because of lice, and oversized utilitarian dress-shirt. *Hogan's Alley* installments often commented on the very events that filled the surrounding newspaper pages, albeit recast with raucous youth and relocated to the poor, working-class section of the prototypical American city. These shrewd, offensive youths simultaneously challenged and indulged ideological assumptions of class, youth, race, and gender. Indeed, in terms of race and ethnicity, Sari Edelstein points out the problematic legacy of *Hogan's Alley* and other early comics, affirming that "while newspapers cultivated their immigrant readerships, they published and circulated cartoons in which immigrants were caricatured and vulgarized" (122). In this process, the children of *Hogan's Alley* display their artifice, as well as the permeability of childhood and the absolutism of creative and social construction.

The figure of the Yellow Kid symbolically renders the relationship I discern between American children's literature and journalism of the late nineteenth and early twentieth centuries. The *Hogan's Alley* published in the same July 26 *World* issue carrying the spectacle of the Populist Party convention and the hyperbolic rhetoric describing Dr. Maximilian M. Weil's unfortunate incident presents a theater scene, "The Opening of the Hogan's Alley Roof Garden" (Outcault Plate 28) (see figure I.1). This illustration presents multiple layers of metanarrative and cultural criticism through the image of coarse, crude city children performing the roles of adult stage actors and members of refined theater society. It underlines the performative, constructed idea not only of American childhood and adulthood, but of white society and the newspaper itself through the artifice of the colored panel and the theater setting. A girl clad in a large Gainsborough hat and balletic costume sings out to the audience from the stage while, unbeknown to her, her tutu catches fire from a stage candle. Next to the smoldering singer, two boys in ridiculously oversized suit coats and fake beards appear to be imitating politicians, indicated by the American flag propped atop one of their heads. The artificiality of each performance stands obvious and unmasked for the audience. Indeed, it is someone from the audience who yells to the girl that her skirt is on fire, thus breaking any pretense of an authentically rendered reality. Rather than lending a sense of authenticity to their roles, the stage costumes worn by the boys only further signal that they are actively creating absurdist entertainment. "The Opening of the Hogan's Alley Roof Garden" successfully erodes presupposed barriers between make-believe and truth, fact and fantasy. Moreover, ignorance of artifice's naturalness and nature's artifice will burn you—just as it does the smoldering singer engrossed in song. Underscoring all this is the Yellow Kid himself, Mickey Dugan, positioned in the forefront of the panel wearing a dress-shirt that partially reads, "Say! If me and Liz cant git no seat we kin git upon de stage an do our little turn …" (Outcault Plate 28). Faced with exclusion or marginalization because he cannot obtain theater tickets, the Yellow Kid shrugs it off knowing he can recast and redirect the production, and knowing that there is no real wall between the worlds of the actors and the audience.

The seemingly outlandish, irreverent behavior of the Yellow Kid and his fellow street urchins so resonated with New Yorkers that its "multitudes … snapped up the growing numbers of Yellow Kid toys, games, cigars, chewing gum, candy, and comic pins to be found in novelty stores, tobacco shops, street carnival booths, and other outlets" (Blackbeard 46). American journalism legend maintains that the Yellow Kid helped spur the great newspaper war between Pulitzer's *World* and William Randolph Hearst's *Journal* after Hearst lured Outcault away from the *World* to ink a new Yellow Kid strip for the *Journal*. Though it is disputed, the Yellow Kid often receives credit for inspiring the term *yellow journalism*, a phrase often used disparagingly to describe progressive-era reporting.[1] Indeed, in 1897, amid the rising turmoil between Spain and Cuba and the growing media presence covering the situation, famed reporter Richard Harding Davis wrote to his mother from Cuba lamenting the "new school of yellow kid journalists" and the ethics of "yellow kid reporters" (Davis, Letter to Mother, Jan. 16, 1897). Academic scholarship often revisits and recontextualizes the "yellow" component of yellow-kid reporting—the bold, sensationalistic maneuvers enacted by turn-of-the-century newspapers—but what about the "kid" part?

Newspaper reporters, as Mark Twain has written in his journals (281), tell our most durable stories, and in children—and literary representations of

Figure I.1. "The opening of the Hogan's Alley roof garden." The New York *World* published this *Hogan's Alley* panel in its July 26, 1896, edition.

children—we find our most curious reporters. I appropriate the popular journalism term "cub reporter," a rookie journalist, to signify the cross-section between children's literature and the newspaper during a time period considered to be a golden age for both, and to show how children function as reporters of artifice.[2] In addition to considering American children's literature as a response, in part, to the rise of the newspaper, I also discern the reciprocity between journalism and children's culture, highlighting how these two realms inform one another through the period's children's literature. In other words, a national ethos finds expression through American children's literature, and children—and our ideas of children—react to and revise these texts. My study looks at work from writers such as Horatio Alger, Jr., L. Frank Baum, and Richard Harding Davis, in addition to examining the children's page of the *Chicago Defender*, first published in 1921. In analyzing selections of the era's children's literature through a contextualization of journalism history, I hope to show how children's literature can operate as social-change agent through its depictions of young people as reporters of artifice.

Journalism and the American Newspaper

The idea of journalism and objective news, the conceit of the newspaper as messenger of fact—these are notions that evolved slowly over the centuries. Indeed, in Europe as far back as the sixteenth century, many eyed the advancement of news *as an industry* with skepticism. Andrew Pettegree points out that "for those traditionally in the know, the industrialization of news, the creation of a news industry where news was traded for profit, threatened to undermine the whole process by which news had been traditionally verified—where the credit of the report was closely linked to the reputation of the teller" (5). Yet this was also the appeal and the power of the news; it democratized knowledge. And for the young democracy of America, the newspaper played a crucial role in establishing a sense of community and national identity. The great strength of the prerevolutionary press in the United States, writes Mitchell Stephens, "was its ability to enfranchise and unify Americans" (190). According to Stephens, the "role of the news in the American Revolution is best understood … as an entirely characteristic exercise in animating and binding a new society, in producing 'a junction' of a majority of the American people" (190). From the 1775 beginning of the war through its six-year stretch, thirty-five newspapers started publication alongside the preexisting thirty-seven outlets (Fellow 59).[3]

After the Revolution, the country continued to "bind" together, to use Stephens's term, through the newspaper, producing a sense of national consciousness. But the press also legitimizes itself through America's formation. "Both the press and the country became established and intertwined during the nineteenth century," assert Betty Houchin Winfield and Janice Hume, who note that the American "press established a separate identity from that in British journals and periodicals" in the century's first decades (129). The century also saw substantial growth in newspaper circulation and outlets, increasing from 235 newspapers in 1801 to 2,600 in 1906 (Winfield 129). Important to understanding the social impact of the newspaper and its reporting choices is the evolution of the press from elite weeklies that served primarily as organs of political parties to the advent of the more accessible penny papers, beginning in the 1830s with the *Sun* and the *Herald* in New York, the *Daily Times* in Boston, and the *Public Ledger* in Philadelphia. Anthony Fellow goes as far to say that after September 3, 1833, the day of the *New York Sun*'s first issue, "a line was crossed in media history, a line that sharply divided the past from the present" (85). "What these papers did," writes Frank Luther Mott, "was to make newspaper readers of a whole economic class" who were previously ignored (*American Journalism* 241). However, as Mott explains, criticism arose that "for the uneducated draymen and porters," newspapers were forced to become more "sensational" than they were for their audiences of "rich merchants" (*American Journalism* 242).[4] With the ostensible democratization of news through the penny press, the newspaper became a means of education and entertainment for families, circulating between parents and children. A contemporary observer remarked of the newspaper, "'Thus the important visitant passes from hand to hand, till every member of the family has gratified his ... curiosity, down to the little children, who ask permission to look at the ships, the houses, or the pictures of the wild beasts that are for exhibition in the menagerie'" (qtd. in Canada 33).

Moreover, the advent of the penny press "changed ... the idea of what news is" because the audience changed, and thus changed the style and content of coverage (Mott *American Journalism* 243). As Karen Roggenkamp astutely points out, "Penny papers of the 1830s and 1840s introduced a new fluidity between literary and journalistic forms in the daily newspaper, a fluidity that functioned even more dramatically two generations later" when the newspapers of Joseph Pulitzer and William Randolph Hearst secured national prominence (1). Over the course of the century, the newspaper required increased craftsmanship and became a form of art in and of itself.

Michael Schudson demonstrates this art from the perspective of reporting, elucidating the way in which our understanding of events, news, and history intersect by detailing how journalistic coverage of the presidential inauguration has changed, a shift that begins to happen in the second half of the nineteenth century. "The changes have to do not with the accuracy of the reporting but with the form in which the report is presented," writes Schudson, explaining that "[e]arly newspapers did not report so much as record" ("Why News Is the Way It Is" 109). The newspaper presented speeches with no interpretation or foregrounding of themes or central issues, "just the full text of the president's message" (109). As the century moved forward, coverage of inaugurations became more of a journalistic endeavor and less one of transcription. "What changed was not recognition of the president's importance," Schudson says, "but rather the idea of what a news story should be and what a reporter should be doing" (110). In doing so, a shift occurred that "reflected not merely a changed political reality" but a reality the newspaper "helped to construct," leading to "a new political world that accepted the news reporter as an interpreter of political events" ("Why News Is the Way It Is" 110).

In addition to the increasing scope of the news reporter's role, the role of advertising took on more weight in the late nineteenth century, with Pulitzer's *World* becoming a business model for other newspapers. "The *World* had become the most profitable newspaper ever published" (Mott *American Journalism* 436) and had "'affected the character of the entire daily press of the country'" according to one observer in 1887 (qtd. in Mott, *American Journalism* 436). But the growing dependence on advertising, as well as the growing industrialization of the country, inevitably altered how newspapers operated and how publishers represented their product. Amy Kaplan writes that because of the success of the department store and a push toward manufactured-goods marketing, newspaper revenue from advertising increased to 55 percent by 1890, up from 44 percent in 1880 (27). "This change meant that the newspaper had to become a kind of advertisement for itself," Kaplan asserts (27). "If the paper's primary goal was to increase circulation in order to sell more products for its advertisers," she says, "it had to present the news in such a way as to advertise itself as a *desirable product*" (Kaplan 27–28; emphasis added). The news became well-coordinated artifice, a choreography between the shrewd talent of reporters and the business savvy of publishers.

In the growing world of journalistic publications in late nineteenth-century America, a variety of genres existed, including dailies, weeklies, and monthlies, each with its own tone and agenda. Into the 1880s, Jonathan Barron notes, a cultural divide appeared between the large metropolitan dailies and some of the prominent weeklies and monthlies (*The Atlantic, Scriber's, Harper's*). Barron argues, "By 1880 the magazines, weekly and monthly, as well as the weekly editions of certain city papers mailed to national subscribers, had created national publications dedicated to genteel values" (20). Using their journalistic positions as opportunities to help shape the nation through a kind of idealism, those in power at these weeklies and monthlies "deliberately and self-consciously asserted their self-appointed role as custodians of character, virtue, and duty," Barron says, writing that the editorial leadership "engaged in a massive campaign of 'cultural evangelism' to promote their ideals through poetry, fiction, and drama" (20).[5]

American journalism itself reacted to the growing power and business of the newspaper. Muckraking journalism both responded to and helped define yellow journalism with its exposés and investigative reporting. Publishers established independent ventures that sought to provide intelligent, thoroughly documented news accounts and narratives; one such was S. S. McClure, who launched *McClure's Magazine* in 1893. *McClure's* featured the groundbreaking work of Ida Tarbell, Lincoln Stephens, William Allen White, and Willa Cather, among others. "'The *story* is the thing,'" said McClure, according to historian Doris Kearns Goodwin (qtd. in Goodwin, xii; emphasis added). "As they educated themselves about the social and economic inequities rampant in the wake of teeming industrialization," Goodwin says, they also "educated the entire country" through their long-form narrative journalism (xii).[6]

The "new journalism" movement of the late nineteenth century endorsed the narrative traditions that Goodwin, Michael Schudson, Karen Roggenkamp, and others describe. Indeed, as Roggenkamp argues, new journalism models itself after fiction, "appropriat[ing] popular literary genres to frame the news for readers" (xv). In recasting "current events into stories laced with the familiar motifs of hoaxes, scientific and travel adventures, mystery and detective tales, and historic romances," newspaper editorial staffs were "in effect revising and resurrecting these popular fictional forms as news items" (Roggenkamp xv). Similarly, the figure of the reporter takes on new cultural significance. In essence, the reporter becomes both the writer and main actor of the ongoing American drama. Schudson describes the shift from the image of the uneducated, hard-drinking "old reporter" to that of the dedicated, spry "new reporter," who usually had attended college (69). The popularity of certain reporters in the 1880s and 1890s—Nellie Bly, Henry Morton Stanley, and Richard Harding Davis, among others—"added greatly to the esprit that attracted young men and more and more young women to the world of journalism" but also showed that "[r]eporters were as eager to mythologize their work as the public was to read of their adventures" (Schudson 69). In the process, the boundaries between artifice and fact become blurred, if there ever were any such distinct boundaries.

Realism and Children's Literature in America

Journalism's prominence in American life during the nineteenth century inevitably embedded itself within literary culture, from Romanticism to realism. "Journalism's presence in the era's literature reflects its presence in American culture," Mark Canada affirms.[7] Canada specifically explores how this presence found expression in antebellum literature, in which newspapers can be found "in the lap of Poe's narrator in 'The Man of the Crowd,' in a volume in Hawthorne's sketch 'Old News,' in the living rooms of Senator Bird and Augustine St. Clair in Stowe's *Uncle Tom's Cabin*," and "[j]ournalists ... appearing in works ranging from Cooper's *Home As Found* to Davis's 'Life in the Iron-Mills'" (31). Near the end of the century, the connection between American literature and journalism evolved into literary realism, a movement that endeavored to accurately depict the experiences and emotions of both the working class and the wealthy, stressing reality and observation over imagination and the ideal.

The shift from the antebellum American romance—described by Nathaniel Hawthorne in his preface to *The House of the Seven Gables* (1851) as a work that should "mingle [in] the Marvelous ... as a slight, delicate, and evanescent flavor" (vii)—to realism occurs in the wake of war and its subsequent scar on the national psyche. This literary transition occurred during a time that saw an economic market produce the ascent of the corporation and the alienation of the wage earner (Wiebe 47). Journalism scholar Thomas B. Connery, who argues that literary realism grew out of a close relationship to journalism through the many realist writers working in both genres, asserts that realism, "a paradigm of actuality," derived from "the observation of life being lived" (15). And "[a]s the century unfolded," Connery explains, "observation involved looking, seeing, and documenting the urban landscape, which became central to the paradigm of actuality" found in realism and journalism (15). Michael Schudson examines the historical changes in journalism and how those changes have affected American perception of reality, in addition to challenging contemporary traditional journalistic conventions, stating that "[w]hile the news story claims to be mimetic, it is in many respects close to the formulaic pole of literary forms" ("Why News Is the Way It Is" 122). "In producing newspapers and television news programs," says Schudson, "journalists are telling stories, and journalists, like everyone else, tell stories according to certain formulae" ("Why News Is the Way It Is" 122). As a result, "Newswriting is governed by narrative patterns imposed not by organizational necessity or ideological purpose but by narrative traditions" (Schudson "Why News Is the Way It Is" 122). As such, journalism *requires* trafficking in artifice.

By the 1880s, the United States saw "an unprecedented market for newspapers" and had "six times as many papers as there had been in the 1860s" (Fishkin 87). Realism as a literary form ostensibly established itself and its concerns for "documenting" an idea of the real lives of Americans with the 1885 publication of former *Atlantic Monthly* editor William Dean Howells's *The Rise of Silas Lapham*. In the realist novel, as opposed to the newspaper article, "slavery, prostitution, racism, economic inequality, and exploitation, the Spanish civil war, political prosecution" could be investigated "with greater freedom" (Fishkin 7). Shelley Fisher Fishkin contends that only "as poets and novelists" could former newspaper writers such as Twain, Theodore Dreiser, and John Dos Passos "transcend" the confines of the newspaper format, enabling them to produce stories that resonated with audiences "in ways their journalism never could," intellectually or emotionally (8).

American literary realism as a means to access Connery's idea of "actuality" demonstrated its own limitations. Indeed, Amy Kaplan illuminates realism's ability to contour reality, describing how "the perceived failure or impossibility of mimesis has led ... critics to chart a more dynamic relation between social and literary structures, one that does not place the text outside society as an imaginative escape, a static window of observation, or a reflecting mirror" (6). Literature and media are not only echo chambers, but also means for mapping and creating meaning in society. Kaplan posits realism's centrality in a "broader cultural effort to fix and control a coherent representation of a social reality that seems increasingly inaccessible, fragmented, and beyond control" (8). Certainly, both realism and the newspaper attempt to help Americans navigate a quickly changing landscape in the late nineteenth century. Their aims sometimes bolstered one another, sometimes vied against each other. "The realist's project to construct a public sphere faced serious competition from the development of the mass media in the 1870s and 1880s," says Kaplan, noting that "Howells's utopian vision of a 'common reality' was already being put into effect by the press, which claimed to purvey ordinary life in the daily newspaper through new categories of reporting such as the 'human interest' story" (25–26). Thus, concurrently answering and guiding economic, social, and technological shifts, novels such as Howells's *Lapham*, which chronicles the rapid financial decline of a fifty-five-year-old Civil War veteran born poor to a farmer in rural Vermont, and later Theodore Dreiser's *Sister Carrie* (1900), project an urban America founded in a morality of the market rather than of the heart. But while "[t]he rise of the modern newspaper is often seen as a popular counterpart to the genesis of literary realism" (Kaplan 26), there is another variable in this cultural equation.

While American realism may have been responding to journalism's ascendancy and limitations, I propose that American children's literature of the time reacts to the newspaper by way of its "cub reporters," or young persons who explore the power and process of artifice through journalism and ventures relating to journalism. Under the guise of mimetic fiction, realism reacts by attempting to further investigate social and psychological realities excluded from journalism's representations. But the texts of children's literature take a different approach by mining journalism's artifice and experimenting with its potential to change social realities. In this, these young persons render themselves reporters of artifice.

The focalization of American anxieties and ideologies through the child during the nineteenth century and beyond repackaged the era's dominant social concerns. In the case of my project, the anxiety is elicited by the newspaper, but scholars have similarly analyzed the ways that other cultural anxieties manifested through the child during the nineteenth and twentieth centuries. For example, in *Racial Innocence* (2011), Robin Bernstein tackles race, deftly arguing that "[c]hildhood innocence ... characterized by the ability to retain racial meanings but hide them under claims of holy obliviousness—secured the unmarked status of whiteness, and the power derived from that status." (8). These "racial meanings" can be found in children's literary and material culture, Bernstein suggests, from Raggedy Ann dolls to Shirley Temple to the relationship between Eva and Topsy in *Uncle Tom's Cabin*. Like Bernstein, I see the child and childhood, through the vehicle of children's literature, responding to broader national conversations while at the same time helping shape and solidify new conversations. In other words, Golden Age children's literature did not exist in a vacuum. It was not passive and was not simply *a response* to cultural anxieties. This relationship was a reciprocal dialogue, and it continues to be so today. Through examining one distinct component of this dialogue, I hope to introduce constructive new ways to think about children's literature. In particular, with the idea of artifice, I want to examine its ability to liberate and activate individual agency when its procedural development is openly acknowledged.

Within the fields of childhood studies and children's literature, productive conversations are happening that force reconsideration of not only what it means to be a child, but also what it means to be human. In her introduction to *The Children's Table: Childhood Studies and the Humanities*, Anna Mae Duane argues that "the study of children ... allows us to rethink the very foundations underlying" our means of social organization, and that "studying childhood requires a radically altered approach to the questions of what constitutes knowledge and what animates the work of power and resistance" (1). Current research within children's and young adult literature research often explores agency—youth's ability to discover "power and resistance." Ever since the 1984 publication of Jacqueline Rose's *The Case of Peter Pan, or the Impossibility of Children's Fiction,* in which Rose posits that children's fiction can only ever be a reflection of the adult and adult desires, scholars have debated the creative autonomy of children. However, while many see children and children's culture as simply reinforcing adult power structures and ideologies, Marah Gubar instead suggests that children's literature of the Golden Age invites child readers to be "collaborators," and that certain canonical and popular works "represent young people as co-producers of texts" (8). Furthermore, such works enable children to "find their own voices despite the existence of preexisting stories about who they are and how they should behave" (Gubar 127). According to Gubar and other scholars such as Victoria Ford Smith, this idea of collaboration continues to permeate children's media and art.

My project intervenes to contend that the cultural response to American journalism seen in children's literature during the Golden Age functions not just as a response, but additionally triggers an ongoing conversation between journalism and children's culture. Given the subtext and context of writers working during the dominance of the newspaper, their texts for children also communicate the reality of and possibility for artifice. Such liberation invites Gubar's coproduction and collaboration, which is then absorbed by literature and popular culture. Though initially a rejoinder to nineteenth-century journalism, American children's literature of the Golden Age and beyond becomes an active agent in shaping how we define childhood. This very process itself reveals the pliancy of such definitions. In his theoretical and critical discussions of epic theater, Bertolt Brecht compares mediums such as "the stage" and "the press" to "apparati" that "impose their views as if it were incognito," thus lulling their audiences into social and political complacency (34). But the adult-author filter of children's literature obviates its ability to go "incognito"; the child-disguise does not fully fit the adult author. To this end, scholars such as Jack Zipes and Rose argue that there really is no such thing as children's literature, with Rose positing that

> Children's fiction is impossible. Not in the sense that it cannot be written (that would be nonsense), but that it hangs on ... the impossible relation between adult and child. Children's fiction sets up a world in which the adult comes first (author, maker, giver) and the child comes after (reader, product, receiver), but where neither of them enter the space in between. (1–2)

However, such a disconnect broadcasts itself; children's literature, impossible or not, validates Brecht's notion of epic theater in that it cannot go "incognito." Its texts absorb these contradictions between child and adult, truth and fantasy, ideal and real so as to expose and celebrate and challenge the facts that surround us, those facts so prized, policed, and pursued during journalism's period of professionalization beginning after the Civil War.

Of course, all fiction engages with generic or social "apparati" and its own relationship with reality to some extent, perhaps especially in the cases of fantasy and absurdist literature. (And indeed, genres that use overt forms of artifice—fantasy, comics, graphic novels, animated films and televisions series—are often associated with or marketed toward children and teenagers.) But *Cub Reporters* specifically questions what it means to have young people cast as reporters of artifice in works of Golden Age children's literature.

The Intersections of American Children's Literature and Journalism

Cub Reporters includes American children's texts of the late nineteenth or early twentieth centuries that deal with reporting and newspaper production. The authors considered here had varying degrees of professional involvement with journalism. By looking at newspaper-centric texts, I mean to distill the reciprocity between journalism and children's literature (and, by proxy, culture)—the ways in which these two realms inform one another. However, I do see the cub reporters of artifice extending beyond newspaper-centric examples of children's literature. The rise of American fantasy and comics in the twentieth century, in addition to narratives that detail youth-directed empirical searches for knowledge, namely detective stories, extend from my argument in the ways that they overtly deconstruct and reassemble social artifice through creative artifice. In this sense, I hope the ideas presented here prove applicable to the ways we think about children's and YA literature more broadly, but my aim is also to expand the ways we talk about, legislate, and educate the lives of young people. Perhaps most importantly, I would like *Cub Reporters* to contribute to the ongoing academic scholarship, cultural conversations, and public engagement seeking to empower young people themselves.

I begin by looking at the cultural place of the newspaper in the late nineteenth century—or, more specifically, those young people who delivered and edited the newspaper headlines to the public. When considering turn-of-the-century children's literature and newspapers, it is impossible to ignore Horatio

Alger, Jr. Yet the rags-to-riches mythos of Alger's novels has overshadowed many of the historical nuances his works present. Chapter 1, "Carrying the Banner: Horatio Alger, the Newsboy, and the Paper," explores the historical and fictional construction of the newsboy, a figure who embodies the relationship between the newspaper and the child and challenges ideologies of power.

Chapter 2 moves on to think about the figure of the reporter. Perhaps the most recognized newspaper reporter of his day, Richard Harding Davis found early success with a string of widely read stories that illustrate newspaper life and the art of reporting. In "Making News and Faking Truth: Richard Harding Davis, the Reporter, and American Youth," I discuss how and to what ends writer-reporter Davis conflates the romanticized ideals of the child and the reporter in his popular stories "Gallegher: A Newspaper Story" (1890) and "The Reporter Who Made Himself King" (1891), stories that feature and were read by young people.

In chapter 3, I'm interested in considering how the ideas of artifice, journalism, and children's literature operate in terms of specific cultural ideologies. Here, I explore how artifice contributes to the social progress of feminist thinking. L. Frank Baum, author of *The Wonderful Wizard of Oz* and another turn-of-the-century newspaperman (albeit a failed one), often alludes to newspaper production in his novels, especially in his popular fiction for girls. "A Spectacle of Girls: L. Frank Baum, Women Reporters, and the Man Behind the Screen in Early Twentieth-Century America" looks at the ways Baum's girl series, *Oz*, and the work of turn-of-the-century women journalists inform and reflect one another through their use of the artifice of spectacle.

After examining the cultural work of artifice in children's novels, I consider how actual children become reporters of and for artifice through interaction with the newspaper. "Join the Club: African American Children's Literature, Social Change, and the Chicago Defender Junior" takes a different approach than previous chapters, given the lack of literature written specifically for black children and the intense racial disparity faced by African Americans during (and after) the first decades of the twentieth century. Here, I suggest that through the acknowledged artifice of the *Chicago Defender*, a newspaper with a stated objective to promote racial equality, its previously overlooked children's page, the Chicago Defender Junior, operates as a form of children's literature—one *written by children*—and contributes to the development of black youth identity.

To conclude, I move forward to the 1960s to address the ways in which the relationship between children's literature, journalism, and artifice evolves through the emerging school of the twentieth century's New Journalism and texts such as Louise Fitzhugh's *Harriet the Spy* (1964). The novel shows Harriet determining her sense of identity through her continuous spying—or reporting—and her writing. She attempts to "know everything" by uncovering artifice and the boundaries of observable fact, which she works through and redefines in her notebook. Meanwhile, Tom Wolfe, unofficial spokesman for New Journalism, makes clear that while writers of New Journalism "were moving beyond the conventional limits of journalism," it was "not merely in terms of technique," but also their manner of reporting—one that "was more intense, more detailed, and certainly more time-consuming than anything that newspaper or magazine reporters, including investigative reporters, were accustomed to" (20–21). Thus, while the writing of Wolfe and others in the early 1960s served as a harbinger for a new period in American journalism—and indeed, American culture—so too does *Harriet* function as a new representation of the child and children's literature.

Much of the work undertaken by humanities scholars today strives to understand hegemonic ideology and unexamined cultural constructions along the lines of gender, race, and class. However, the growing field of childhood studies forces us to also examine our assumptions about youth, age, and agency, and the ways in which these assumptions affect the human condition. Because childhood—as we currently conceive it—plays a central role in our individual lives, its scholarly study must be part of academic conversations and research within the humanities. Through examining how American children's literature recalibrates the use of artifice in response to the newspaper's societal dominance, I attempt to similarly recalibrate the ways in which the academy and culture think about children's literature and childhood. By destabilizing how we understand ideas of childhood and its cultural production, we are able to assess our current segregation of child and adult spheres and reconsider the ways in which we accept or challenge prevailing ideologies.

When, in the July 26, 1896, *Hogan's Alley* panel, the Yellow Kid tells us he can "git upon de stage an do our little turn," he subtly alludes to the persuasive power that the concepts of the child and the newspaper both possess because of their associations with novelty. Indeed, the conceit of newness forever links the symbolic work of the child to that of journalism, each derived out of the ability to express and experience that which is new. Mickey Dugan reminds us that the figure of the child and the idea of the newspaper, defined by their newness, reiterate the human capacity to learn and create continually, again and again, be it an artistic "little turn," tomorrow's edition of the newspaper, or entire cultural belief systems.

And so, I now echo those newsboys of the American imagination: "Extra! Extra! Read all about it."

Chapter 1

Carrying the Banner

Horatio Alger, Jr., the Newsboy, and the Paper

In August 2014, the Tony Award-winning Broadway musical *Newsies* ended its run at the Nederlander Theatre after "1005 performances, attendance of more than 1 million and a gross of over $100M" thanks in large part to its "fiercely devoted fans" ("BREAKING NEWS: NEWSIES to Close"). Those fans, it turns out, include adults who were children and teenagers when the stage musical's source material—a 1992 major motion picture from Disney that was a critical and box-office failure—reached cult status through the power of VHS and soundtrack cassette tapes. At a pre-Broadway performance of the stage show in 2011, thirty-two-year-old Heather Allen told *The Daily Beast*, "When I was little, we would have sleepovers and listen to the tape over and over again, and write down the songs" (Setoodeh). But Broadway's *Newsies* has also produced a new generation of young fans. A simple YouTube search yields seemingly countless tributes from child and teenage "fansies," a legion of fresh-faced *Newsies* enthusiasts. In one such video from April 2014, a small boy performs his own rendition of a song from the show and film, "Carrying the Banner," complete with choreography, a makeshift set of the newsboys' lodging house and New York streets constructed from dining-room chairs, and a wardrobe of a vest, bowler-style hat, and sweatpants (bebesadie) (see figure 1.1). Dancing around the chairs, this small boy chants the words of newsboys from their 1899 strike as imagined by lyricist Jack Feldman—song lyrics inspired by David Nasaw's *Children of the City: At Work and at Play* (1985), according to the cover of the book's 2012 edition.

Just as Heather Allen did when she was a little girl, this boy has probably listened to the catchy rhymes over and over again. He propagates and reinscribes the idea of child ingenuity, as well as children's centrality in shaping the news. For, as the newsies shrewdly sing out, "if [they] hate the headline / [they]'ll make up a headline" because to "move / the next edition," they need "an earthquake or a war" (Feldman, "Carrying the Banner"). Through the lyrics

Figure 1.1. Mattie rehearsing "Carrying the Banner" from Newsies. This image comes from a YouTube video posted by user "bebesadie" in April 2014.

the amateur boy performer sings in his YouTube video, he not only imitates a piece of popular entertainment, but evinces the ways in which American youth culture and journalism have long informed one another.

Written during the time of actual newsboys in the nineteenth and twentieth centuries, Horatio Alger Jr.'s, romanticized depictions of this figure suggest young people's ability to edit or manipulate news narratives by way of "mak[ing] up a headline"—and this long before the term "fake news" became common parlance. In undermining the authority of the newspaper, the newsboy destabilizes traditional power relationships between child and adult, fiction and truth. I look to Alger's newsboy representation specifically because, given Alger's highly prolific career as a writer of American children's fiction in the latter nineteenth century, his numerous renderings of working-class boys have helped shape the public imagination's ideas of Gilded Age street youth (see figure 1.2). Via his newsboy characters, Alger's texts show avenues through which socially disempowered, impoverished young people can find a sense of agency.

More than just selling newspapers to the public, Alger's newsboys (and their *Newsies* descendants) point toward American apprehension about the newspaper's sovereignty given its total control over not only the story of the day, but the national narrative. This chapter looks at how Alger's newsboys—who jointly borrowed from and contributed to the lives of actual newsboys—confront this historical moment. What are the enduring legacies of these literary confrontations, and what do such instances of intersection between the construction of youth identity and national identity imply? The cultural figure of the American newsboy represents a reporter of artifice, a figure who lays bare the scripted, written, malleable qualities of journalistic and social truths. In short, the newsboy unsettles preexisting power dynamics. In the role of artificer, Alger's newsboy recognizes and uses artifice to his advantage, and in the process, challenges the legitimacy of foundational hegemonic structures. To explore the particular cultural work of the newsboy, as well as my broader thematic concerns about the relationship between American children's literature and journalism, I contextualize Alger's texts within the frameworks of the newsboy of the popular imagination, the newsboy in history, and the historical situation of the newspaper.

Alger's *Rough and Ready; or Life among the New York Newsboys* (1869), the novel to which I pay the most attention in this chapter, exemplifies the standard, formulaic Alger novel in terms of plot.[1] The storyline, familiar to readers who have previously encountered any of Alger's other children's books, follows newsboy Rufus and his younger sister Rose as they escape the guardianship of their abusive, alcoholic stepfather and details their subsequent attempt to support themselves in the city. But Alger's novel also portrays the cleverness of the working newsboy, ultimately rendering him as a kind of discerning news reporter. "*Times, Herald, Tribune, World!*" cries fifteen-year-old orphan Rufus (106). He stations himself at his usual corner outside the *Times* building, shouting promises to crowds that pass him by: "All the news that's going, for only four cents! That's cheap enough, isn't it?" (106). Rufus attracts the notice of a possible customer, who buys a *Herald*, and then Rufus tries to whet the man's appetite for the next day's news. He gives the man an exclusive scoop, telling him that "the *Herald* has sent up a reporter to put a big rock on the Erie road, and throw off the afternoon train," and then quickly adds that "the *Times* and *Tribune* are arrangin' to get up some horrid murders. Maybe they'll have 'em in tomorrow's paper. You better come round and buy 'em all" (107). Seemingly beguiled and miffed by the audacity of the boy, the man walks off with his copy of the *Herald*. With the preview of upcoming coverage, newsboy Rufus projects an image of himself as having inside information into the departmental organization of the newspaper's reporting divisions. But he also shows himself to be a businessman, ever-mindful of building his customer base. Equally important, Rufus is probably making up all his supposed journalism intel. This performance allows readers to see Rufus as a reporter of artifice, a role that exposes the unstable boundaries between truth and fiction while simultaneously

Figure 1.2. Ragged Dick series. This illustration was included as a frontispiece for the Ragged Dick series circa 1895.

inviting others to build new, more relevant boundaries. Here, I want to think about the ways in which the creative power of the American newsboy—a term I use that conflates literary and historical accounts of a figure located at the nexus of youth, journalism, and nation—disrupts accepted social narratives of power and identity.

The Newsboy of the Popular Imagination

The late nineteenth and early twentieth centuries, roughly the years between the Civil War and World War I, signal the Golden Age of the newspaper in America, a time when "real authority flowed from the printed word," according to George H. Douglas (vi). These years correspond to the Golden Age of children's literature in the United States and England.[2] Because the newsboy traverses these two golden ages, the figure has been deemed a character indicative of American culture and history. Scholars have made compelling arguments about the newsboy that illuminate and further illustrate how ideologies of class and race manifest through this youth figure. Karen Sanchez-Eppler, using the newsboy as a stand-in for the multiple forms of visible urban-child labor during the nineteenth century, argues that his representation helped enable the growth of a middle class. "[T]hrough depictions of working-class children," Sanchez-Eppler states, "middle-class ideals are first and most forcefully articulated" (154). She reads the "literary use of the newsboy" as a means to "define and value middle-class childhoods through the depiction of their antithesis" (164). And while the myth of the white newsboy looms large, according to Vincent DiGirolamo, the role of the black newsboy in social history and popular culture has been notably neglected, despite—or perhaps because of—the ways in which he personifies the country's difficult negotiations among race, class, and labor. Knowing that the white newsboy "stands as a symbol of personal advancement through industry, honesty, and thrift," black newsboys found themselves in a paradoxical position—that "to get ahead, they must believe in an economic system that has served to keep them down" (63).

I focus on Alger's representations of the newsboy because of the sheer pervasiveness of his works and their tenacious grip on the popular imagination, despite critical disfavor over the course of the twentieth century. Alger, most recognized for *Ragged Dick; or, Street Life in New York with Boot Blacks* (1868), wrote more than one hundred books portraying the lives of poor, working-class boys and their attempts to achieve economic stability. He has been widely criticized not only for his formulaic approach, but also for the books' sensational tone. *Ragged Dick* was

Alger's only true bestseller, with an estimated total of 800,000 copies when Alger died in 1899, but the prolific nature of his writing coupled with the texts' transition from hardback to the dime-novel format made the Alger name universally accessible and abundant (Mott, *Golden Multitudes* 158). Yet by the late 1920s, libraries had started to discard his novels from their collections (Scharnhorst, "Demythologizing Alger" 189). Harold Bloom saw the mocking of Alger as so necessary that he included Nathanael West's Alger satire *A Cool Million* (1934) in *The Western Canon: The Books and School for the Ages* (1996). Carol Nackenoff says the Alger name has taken on a meaning that requires little to no knowledge of his books, that his "name itself is a stand-in for ideas supposedly derived from his fiction" to the extent that "'Horatio Alger' has entered the language and discourse of daily life" (3). Scholarship, such as that from Gary Scharnhorst and Michael Moon, has done much to dispel the notion that Alger's fiction offers a simplistic rags-to-riches myth. Scharnhorst and Moon underscore the requirement that wealthy patrons appear in most of the stories, in addition to observing that the boy characters generally ascend to more-or-less middle-class status, not affluence. Nevertheless, the ensuing figure of Alger and the rags-to-riches myth continues to overshadow many of the historical nuances his works present.

While morality and didacticism dominate Alger's fiction, those qualities do not exclude it from providing insight into late nineteenth-century America. Glenn Hendler sees Alger working to shape a vision for the United States, and he compares Alger's literary motivation to that of Frederick Law Olmstead's architectural aspirations. Hendler "read[s] Horatio Alger's novels and the responses they provoked, like the controversies over Olmsted's plans for Central Park, as moments in the struggle to shape the American public sphere, in particular to define the roles men and boys were to play in the economic market and the mass-cultural public" (416). Undoubtedly, there is a "shap[ing]" component to the Alger canon; Hendler puts forward that "Alger's narrative formula is designed to enlist his readers in the construction of a literary counterpart to the ideal realm of leisure, discipline, and genteel performance Olmsted envisioned" (416). Alongside literature and architecture, the "construction" of an American "ideal realm" to which Hendler refers also occurred through journalism. Newspapers, each selling its own vision of America, proliferated during the last half of the century, with "American newspapers increas[ing] in number by one third in the decade of the sixties, so that there were about 4,500 of them by 1870" (Mott, *American Journalism* 404). As I will soon show, Alger's newsboy, well aware of and financially dependent on journalism's influence, demonstrates the ways in which this influence itself can be shaped—and that young people can be the shapers.

The Newsboy of History

By the middle of the nineteenth century, the newsboy had become a recognized feature on the stage of the American city.[3] In an 1854 edition of Philadelphia's *North American and United States Gazette*, an anonymous writer addresses the issue of these urban actors.[4] "The city newsboys are a peculiar class of our local population, and attract no small share of the attention of strangers from the interior," the writer remarks ("The City Newsboys Are a Peculiar Class" n.p.). These boys—some astonishingly young, some in their late teens, and many orphaned—broadcasted the headlines of a still-bourgeoning America in an attempt to sell the day's newspaper and support themselves or their struggling families. In their boisterousness and audacity, and sometimes in their outlandishness, the pitches from this "peculiar class" of youths arguably defined part of the nineteenth-century metropolitan landscape. The *Gazette* writer acknowledges that while newsboys are "[u]seful enough in their ways," they ostensibly "contrive" headlines, spectacle, and sales "by their clamor" in the "throng they keep up at a few particular points, and the deceptions they practice," and that, too often, the newsboys "make themselves the subjects of frequent anathemas" (n.p.). Underlining the notion that such public acts of sensationalism are distinctly American, the writer maintains that in "England, where the people are, as a general thing, slow, careful, and methodical such frauds could not prove successful to any extent" (n.p.).

Certainly, these "deceptions" and "frauds" of newsboys incensed some, but the intelligence and skill put into the performance of selling their newspapers fascinated many. A piece entitled "Ragged Newsboys of New York" published in an 1852 *New Hampshire Statesman* describes newsboys as "a class of the most cunning, wide-awake, indefatigable, industrious, noisy little urchins that grace the streets of any city" who "make the air vocal with their shrill and not unmusical cries" (n.p.). The writer here praises the work ethic and talent of these "urchins," interpreting any notion of "fraud" as simply part of their required business "tactics" (n.p.). Indeed, their "not unmusical cries" become a soundtrack for the city that only intensifies the mystique of the American metropolis in the last half of the nineteenth century, for "strangers and visitors are as much struck with the characteristics of the newsboys as they are with the bustle and activity of our population, or the appearance of our streets and buildings" (n.p.). These newsboy "cries," whether exaggerated or fabricated, present the potential to influence the hearer's sense of community, culture, and nation. And, given newsboys' association with "clamor," it would seem that many could not avoid hearing of the multiple visions of America that they created through their "cries."

In his history of the American newspaper, Frank Luther Mott describes newsboys as more than just vendors. He likens them to crucial, overlooked cogs in development of journalism, affirming that in the period between 1833 and 1860, the "[h]umblest of the journalists were the newsboys" (314). He calls these young "journalists" a "heterogeneous, loud-voiced, shrewd lot" and points out that the "ragged, shouting, insistent New York newsboy of the 1830's [sic] was something new in the world" (314). Mott himself does not seem to know whether this image of the newsboy—one often associated with the newsboy's efforts to support himself (and possibly a parent or sibling) and climb the economic ladder—is a fact or an idea derived from "edifying novels and plays" (314), further evidence of the mutual, concurrent process of art and life shaping one another and ideological frameworks. But if we latch on to Mott's assertion that the newsboy was the "humblest of the journalists," with journalists and newspapers reflecting the story of the nation, we are prodded into considering the impact and meaning of the story coming from the newsboy, this child journalist, and the value of his role.[5]

The Newsboy and Reporting Artifice

Alger's Rufus illustrates the necessity and basic "truth" of artifice, showing how it can be used as a means to achieve agency, and how it is used to create a shared idea of reality. He nullifies his act of headline fabrication by saying that the newspaper does the same thing—editors engage in artifice. Rufus decides to follow the leading paradigm of journalism that he discerns. If the newspaper can invent, so can he. The text privileges the newsboy's innovative capacity while at the same time positioning young people as symbolic reporters of American identity. In telling fellow newsboy Johnny to publicize the explosion of a steamboat, Rufus draws upon sensationalism and the idea of America as not only a growing, prosperous nation, but also one of spectacle. The image of the steamboat in the nineteenth century correlates to the country's westward expansion, evolving trade, and increasing wealth. That Rufus's fictitious boat did not just explode, but "sent five hundred people thrown half a mile high in the air!" (11), enables the story to generate the most extreme visual possible as this enormous vessel morphs into a raging fire shooting masses of bodies far into the sky. Rufus actively participates in generating the notion that America is a nation without discretion, yet also one that is extraordinary, for one man "miraculously" gets saved (11). Through his outrageous headlines, Rufus circulates the message of America as spectacle into public consciousness.

Rufus understands the newspaper's influence. He likewise knows that journalism is a craft and requires artifice, a requirement that enables sensationalistic practices but also engenders more sophisticated reporting and coverage. Logically following the country's growth in the latter nineteenth century is the growth of journalism, as it works to reflect the evolving American story as well as direct it and provide a sense of national identity. The expansion of the newspaper industry—an upsurge of 222 percent from 1870 to 1890 (Douglas 83–84)—thus necessitated a different kind of newsroom. With increasing readerships and budgets, "editors came to rely less on ... informal sources of news and more on free-lance writers and hired reporters who wrote for pay," according to Michael Schudson (65). Mott describes this time as a changeover from a single editor running a one-man show to larger, more skilled staffs operating with reporters who cover individual beats (*American Journalism* 546). Stephen Banning notes that "journalistic professionalization started well before the twentieth century" and was "part of a gradual process, rather than a phenomenon that appeared suddenly after 1900 with the proliferation of professional associations, schools, and codes of ethics" (157). Even before the turn of the century, the global community took note of American journalism's strength when a "writer in an English magazine declared in 1893: 'There are better reporters in America than anywhere else in the world'" (Mott, *American Journalism* 603). The improving skill of the reporter helped fortify American journalism's ability to document the news of the young country while also enabling the newspaper's capacity to create and sell national narratives.[6]

In the "Printing and Publishing" section of the *Twelfth Census of the United States* (1902), William S. Rossiter notes the technological advances of the industry over the previous decades, such as the move from "imperfect, poor" cotton rags to wood pulp, "factors which must not be neglected in any careful survey of the advance of printing" (52). Rossiter also comments on the public's increased appetite for news, which stemmed from the newspaper industry's enhanced capabilities to produce it efficiently and effectively. "Partly because of the ambitious and progressive spirit of the period, and partly because of the lavish expenditures of capital made by reorganized or newly established publications in order to break into the patronage of prosperous competitors and sure a foothold," Rossiter explains, "the dailies of the great cities became the purveyors of the news of the world to an extent never before attempted. In many cases—especially New York city [sic]" (53). This seeming windfall of information into the urban public sphere filters, for many, through the newsboy.

In unpacking the significance of the newsboy as depicted in Alger, the texts suggest the faultiness of a binary distinction between truth and romance, art and news, journalism and fiction—and even that of child and adult—because of the newsboy's capacity to offer expression to all. Mark Canada, in outlining the relationship between early American fiction and journalism, states that the two "emerged in the nineteenth century as two distinct disciplines, each with its own set of aims, conventions, and practices, as well as, most significantly, its own sense of truth" (3). Alger's free-agent newsboys bridge this divide and make us further question the ways in which turn-of-the-century children's literature constructs truth in response to journalism's growth, and how these strands help weave together the larger cultural web defining American childhood and identity.

Alger, the Real and the Romantic

Despite his label as an author of rote yet sensationalized plots and characterizations, Alger saw himself as a reporter of the conditions of working boys—a more truthful reporter than those working at the newspapers, because he could effect social change through emotional resonance. In the introduction to the *Ragged Dick* follow-up *Fame and Fortune, or, The Progress of Richard Hunter* (1868), Alger writes, "The volumes might readily be made more matter-of-fact, but the author has sought to depict the inner life and represent the feelings and emotions of these little waifs of city life" (n.p.). Gary Scharnhorst explains that shortly after he moved to New York City in 1866, "Alger began to study the habits and to visit the habitats" of the city's poor working children, such as the Newsboys' Lodging House (77). Alger's *Fame and Fortune* introduction implies the author's recognition of the reciprocal relationship between art and life, because he "hopes thus to excite a deeper and more widespread sympathy in the public mind" through his careful study of and reporting on poor children (n.p.). Alger picked up the behaviors of newspaper reporting through his visits and interviews with, and subsequent writing about, street children, but he also used the newspaper to further inform his plots and characterizations of street boys. "I met the hero of 'Rough and Ready' at the Newsboys' Lodge, in the upper part of the old 'Sun' building," writes Alger in the 1890 *Ladies Home Journal* article "Are My Boys Real?" (123). He also details how he depends on the newspaper: "I am often indebted for characters and incidents to paragraphs in the daily press.... I have no hesitation in saying that it would be quite impossible for me to write half the number if I had not drawn in large part my characters and material from real life" (123–24).[7] Through his child protagonists, Alger speaks to the period's culture, which is invested in rendering the presentation of facts. And through his mastering of artifice, Alger's newsboy reports youth's ability to manipulate facts and subvert power.

Alger's use of the newsboy as reporter of artifice through active engagement with it first appears in *Ragged Dick*. Orphaned, streetwise Dick supports himself through boot blacking, but has dabbled in multiple trades, including selling newspapers. This "ragged" incarnation of the newsboy, which arises after the first newsboys appear following the New York *Sun*'s advertisement for street vendors in 1833 (Douglas 7), fits with the typical characterization made of this group as "homeless lads ... spending nights in empty barrels and packing-boxes or crouched over sidewalk gratings," who "were up at daybreak and hollered the news, peddled, or polished shoes for money for food, tobacco, and drink" (Bartow 255). To push his sales during his stint as newsboy, Dick yells the false headline "Great news! Queen Victoria assassinated!" (34). Of all the sensationalized news stories to invent, Dick broadcasts the "great" fortuitous proclamation that a monarch has not only died, but been murdered, insinuating revolt and perhaps revolution. This "great news," however false, helps increase sales and profit, as "all" of Dick's "Heralds went off like hot cakes" (34). Alger forces the image of a toppled monarch again when Dick asks "another boy what the paper said," to which the boy fallaciously tells Dick the "King of Africa was dead" (68). In essence, these newsboys bolster a procapitalist nation through shouting their headlines that condemn kingship and disseminate democracy, for as Schudson has noted, "[m]odern journalism ... had its origins in the emergence of a democratic market society" (57).

With *Rough and Ready*, Alger presents a fuller exploration of the newsboy trade, one in which Rufus, similar to Dick, edits and invents news to sell papers. Alger's narrator, however, notes that Rufus, "while a favorite of mine, for his energy, enterprise, and generous qualities" does not "represent" a "model boy." The existence of the "model boy" cannot be found in "real life," the narrator says, though Rufus "has grown up to be a pretty good boy" (12). Here, in a strange move, the narrator implicitly condemns "real life" because its conditions necessarily eradicate model boys. If the world of the novel, Alger's New York City, revolves around the circulation of the newspaper—a circulation not only of capital, but also "real life" news that the text deems inadequate—what might the text be suggesting about American journalism and the child's ability to co-opt it?

The newsboy profession in Alger's novels functions as an accessible entry point into the labor force through which the diligent boy can earn a wage and get a unique education. Frank, the central character in *The Telegraph Boy* (1887), first makes his living as a newsboy and later relies on the skills and lessons acquired during his time selling papers. When looking for a telegraph-delivery address, Frank's "knowledge of the city, gained from the walks he took when a newsboy, made it easy for him to find the place of which he was in search" (116). Before he secures a spot "smashing" luggage in *Ben the Luggage Boy* (1870), Ben gets his start as a newsboy thanks to the suggestion and start-up funds from a sympathetic newspaper reporter. Even after he lands a more prosperous position, Ben knows he can return to the reliable post of newsboy, if need be. *The Errand Boy; or, How Phil Brent Won Success* (1888) finds the title character dismissed from his job, and before the helpful Mr. Carter declares he will intervene on the boy's behalf to get his job back, Phil had decided "to sink his pride and go into business as a newsboy the next day" (though the "very unexpected arrival of Mr. Carter put quite a new face on matters") (154). Selling newspapers, while ultimately romanticized, was still, after all, a low-paying, low-rung position on the economic ladder.

The most prominent example of the Alger's newsboy hero, Rufus—or Rough and Ready, a name "gained … partly from his resemblance in sound to his right name of Rufus, but chiefly because it described him pretty well" (16)—complicates both the idea of the delinquent, ragamuffin newsboy responsible for the "frequent anathemas" mentioned by the *Gazette* writer and the concept of the honest boy hero. A similar tension exists with the text's portrayal of industry (in both the corporate and individual senses of the word), which it both values and maligns. Rufus, while a "good boy" who is "strictly honest" and protects younger sister Rose from their alcoholic and abusive stepfather, participates in deceitful practices to engage potential newspaper customers (16, 71). The text tries to reconcile Rufus's duplicity on the job with his otherwise model morality by making his tactics support an ideal of American industry—the same ideals and exploits of capitalism practiced by the papers he sells. The text continually aligns the actions of the newspaper with those of the newsboy. The *Herald*, for example, is "the most enterprising paper in America," and newsboys are among the "most enterprising street boys … capitalists to a small amount" (9, 13). The choice of "enterprising" suggests a certain kind of innovation while connoting business and profit, which is what we see from Rufus when he is selling papers or helping his fellow workplace colleagues. During a scene in which Rufus struggles to teach lazy Johnny Nolan to be a newsboy, Johnny asks Rufus what headlines he should yell out. "Steamboat exploded on the Mississippi! Five hundred people thrown half a mile high in the air! One man miraculously saved by falling in a mud hole!" Rufus tells Johnny to shout (11). Johnny goes off to relate "the remarkable news which had just been communicated to him," leaving Rufus pleased at his knack for mentoring novice newsboys.

The abilities demonstrated here show the newsboy's capacity to function as both editor and reporter. In making up the headline about the steamboat, Rufus assigns the story, as an editor would, but he also is the reporter; he creates the content for Johnny to sell. And even if people do not buy Johnny's papers, they will hear his cries and probably accept some or all of it as truth. As Rufus sends Johnny off, he knows he has created a good story that will get Johnny customers: "'That ought to sell the papers,' said Rough and Ready to himself. 'Anyway, Johnny's got it exclusive. There ain't any other newsboy that's got it'" (11). Later, after Johnny indeed sells all his papers, he asks Rufus, "[W]as that true about the steamboat?" (12). Rufus expertly replies, "Well, if it isn't true now, it will be some other day.... Anyhow, it isn't any worse for us to cry news that ain't true, than for the papers to print it when they know it's false" (12). Like a veteran editor or reporter on a beat, Rufus believes he has learned the nature of American news, justifying his actions by explaining that a steamboat explosion will *eventually* happen. Instead of reporting factual truth, the child-figure shows his skillful handling of artifice, a different kind of truth. This scene conveys a cultural ambivalence about the institution of the newspaper. While it promulgates the newspaper's powerful societal role, it also emphasizes its potential for fraudulence. But in showing Rufus creating his own news and openly acknowledging the truth of such handiwork, *Rough and Ready* recasts the child newsboy as a reporter of—and for—artifice.

The Cultural Performance of the Newsboy

An article published in a 1900 edition of Charleston's *The Sunday State* discusses the "evolution of the newsboy," remarking that the young workers have shown an "increasing display of politeness" and excellent "conduct of their business," always "remembering what papers their customers take" (4). The writer of this piece attributes "energy and intelligence" to the updated newsboy, namely for his ability to efficiently get newspapers put into the hands of all his clients. The "art" of this "modern" newsboy depends on his ability to navigate and manage the crowd; depicted as standing tall amid a "rushing tide," the writer valorizes him for weathering the storm of the modern city and those impatient readers ready for the day's news (4). His mobility and quick thinking in passing the correct paper to his regular customers win him admiration. The "evolution" points to developments in the newspaper industry—American workers begin to prefer the afternoon newspaper edition, forcing the routine of the newsboy to follow suit (Nasaw 62–63)—as well as to changes resulting from regulations regarding child labor and education. However, the described "evolution" also suggests a cultural osmosis of Alger's plucky-yet-polite boy through this courteous, artful reincarnation, a suggestion supported by David Nasaw's assertion that newsboys "were avid Alger fans" (60). The "evolution" of the newsboy arguably exhibits itself in Alger's later stories, which drift away from depictions of brash nineteenth-century newsboys "reporting" artifice by means of the text showing their participation in journalistic invention. Rather, these later stories seemingly comment on the influential cultural role of the newsboy in addition to "reporting" other modes of artifice that enable the title characters to achieve agency.

Alger published *Dan, the Detective* in 1884, though it later carried the title *Dan, the Newsboy*. Here, the text presents a sanitized newsboy, one only rarely seen creating audacious headlines. Dan's standard cry runs along the lines of "*Evening Telegram*! Only one left. Going for two cents, and worth double the money. Buy one, sir?" (9). He draws attention to the name of the paper, the quantity left, and the price; he stresses the deal rather than the contents of the newspaper because by this time, the public knows what they are purchasing. But Dan still must do some wily wheedling. After he makes his plea for the *Telegram*, he entices a customer through his "business-like tone" (9). A "gentleman" approaches Dan as "he was ascending the steps of the Astor House" and says, "You seem to appreciate the *Telegram*, my boy. Any important news this afternoon?" (9). Dan replies, "Buy the paper, and you'll see" (9). Though Dan portrays the characteristic newsboy spunk, his story, as with the protagonist of *Luke Walton; or the Chicago Newsboy* (1889), interests itself much less in the newsboy trade. As the original title implies, Dan would rather engage in detective work, which, through unmasking contrivance by way of reconstructing criminal plots, displays an engagement with and exposure of artifice similar to that of newsboy work.

Perhaps the most curious of Alger's newsboy novels in its strange metanarrative of late-nineteenth-century publishing and in its romanticization of the newsboy is *Ben Bruce: Scenes in the Life of a Bowery Newsboy* (1901), first serialized from 1892 to 1893 in Frank Munsey's magazine *The Golden Argosy*. In the novel, Ben runs away from his country home and cruel stepfather to New York, where he begins work as a newsboy.[8] During a stop in Boston before he continues to New York, Ben manages to save the life of a young boy (who, of course, has a wealthy, grateful father) from being mauled by a mad dog. Following this, a *Boston Globe* reporter approaches Ben to get a better account of the incident and a photograph to include in the paper. For Ben, the validation of recognition from the newspaper gives him legitimacy, and "[h]e felt that it was quite the most wonderful day in his life" (67). The newspaper effectively assists Ben in crafting a new identity for himself. He even gets to hear his story shouted back at him before he leaves for New York when a newsboy calls out, "Evenin' papers! *Record* and *Globe*! All about the mad dog!" (73).

When the story introduces a particularly odd character, the aspiring writer Sylvanus Snodgrass (a hilarious self-parody of Alger, whether intentional or not),[9] it underscores the period's literary debate between fiction and journalism and their respective cultural roles. Snodgrass educates Ben in the true writer's *raison d'être*: "'[M]oney is not everything. I hope to acquire fame, to live in the hearts of future generations'" (91). The pretentious Snodgrass, who frequently submits short stories to the literary weeklies, has a fascinating preoccupation with *Atlantic* editor William Dean Howells.[10] Ben replies to Snodgrass that he thinks Howells makes good money on his novels, to which Snodgrass quips, "'There isn't excitement enough in his productions,'" seeing as they "'lack snap and fire'" (91). The daily newspapers and their newsboys (as well as Snodgrass's sensational tales) depend on the "snap and fire"—such as mad dogs nearly killing children—that Snodgrass believes the literary realism of Howells omits, highlighting the tension between realistic fiction and sensational journalism of the late nineteenth century.

As the novel unfolds, it notably concerns itself with artifice in relation to the notion of truthful representation. After Ben begins work as a newsboy, his fine suit (a gift from the father of the boy whom Ben saved) becomes a source of contention between him and the other veteran newsboys:

> "Patsy," said Mike, "did you take notice of that dude that's sellin' papers near Houston Street?"
>
> "Yes, Patsy, the one that's dressed like a Fifth Avenue swell."
>
> "Yes, he's the one."
>
> "Don't he put on style, though? I never dressed like him."
>
> "Thrue [sic] for you, Mike, nor I either." (129–30)

The newsboys initially challenge Ben's authenticity as a newsboy because of his expensive attire, but in the midst of doing so, they begin to wonder about their own rights to the role. Patsy and Mike have "never dressed like" Ben. Yet might Ben, through his performance of what he thinks a newsboy is and his fancy suit-costume, be more authentic? Ben is, after all, "a boy of spirit," and soon enough he proves himself at the job (132). The text further stresses the slipperiness between art and life when Ben earns the role of a newsboy in a stage performance at the Bowery, signifying his embodiment of an established cultural trope—one that the author himself helped create. After his first performance, Mike and Patsy accept Ben with "great pride" (154). Only after his being is replicated through art does Ben seem to become relevant to others. He finds a sense of identity through his performance and the subsequent notice of his performance in the newspapers, first with "a paragraph in the *Herald*" and then mention in "the *Sun* and *World*, both of which spoke well of his acting" (156). *Ben Bruce* signals the significance of the newspaper in qualifying identity and essentially obviates the necessity to distinguish between the real and the romantic, or fact from myth, because, ultimately, they subsist on and sustain one another.

Ben Bruce links, quite literally, dramatic performance to cultural performance. With the required token character of "Jed the Newsboy" in the Bowery play, the novel demonstrates how the artifice of performance constructs ideology; after Ben performs the role of newsboy on stage, he earns respect from the other newsboys. The figure of the newsboy, scripted through reality and romance, indeed associates childhood with performativity. However, it also associates young people with a powerful subversive potential. In controlling the news—or at least, influencing what the public thinks the news is—the newsboy finds a kind of agency that could read as thrilling to many. If the newspaper steers American life, then the disenfranchised child stands to gain pleasure from imagining what it would be like to control its message. Of the many reasons why Alger chose to feature newsboys in his novels, there is a very obvious one: children liked reading about them. They wanted to play the role of a newsie then, as they still do today.

The momentum *Newsies* found before its official Broadway opening and the enormous success it garnered afterward may seem counterintuitive. This is the Internet Age—insiders wrote the obituary for the print press long ago, and children have little, if any, nostalgia for physical newspapers since they are probably more familiar with news organizations' social-media feeds or websites. However, youths' ability to insert themselves into and redirect the wider national message will always be an attractive idea, writes Ramin Setoodeh in his 2011 piece for *The Daily Beast*. "[F]or many of the kids who watched *Newsies* growing up, what was so appealing was the way in which the movie empowered its young protagonists," says Setoodeh (n.p.). That allure continues today. From Alger's audiences to the young boy reenacting scenes from *Newsies*, these American children indicate their desire to not just carry the banner, but to create it.

Chapter 2

Making News and Faking Truth

Richard Harding Davis, the Reporter,
and American Youth

In March of 1893, reporter and author Richard Harding Davis wrote to his mother, fellow writer and editor Rebecca Harding Davis, from Cairo. The prominent twenty-eight-year-old correspondent was touring the Mediterranean for a *Harper's Weekly* series in which he planned to document the people, cities, and landscape of the region, a venture that would be similar in fashion to his previous American West series.[1] In the letter, he initially jokes with his mother about his fame and the peculiarity of seeing his book *Gallegher and Other Stories* (1891) for sale in a Cairo shop, especially because one of the book's short stories references foreign travel to Cairo. But Davis soon becomes more serious, calling into question not only his ability to accurately render Cairo and the other places on his travels, but also his right to do so. "It is an immense city and intensely interesting especially the bazaars but you feel so ignorant about it all that it really angers you," Davis tells his mother, adding that he is "disappointed so far in the trip because it has developed nothing new beyond the fact that going around the world is of no more importance than going to breakfast" (Letter to Mother, March 11). Davis, perhaps understandably, finds frustration in his geographic and cultural unfamiliarity. But he is also frustrated with the seeming ubiquity of foreign travel. With so many people now traveling to foreign destinations, how can his writing add to the experience in a way that feels both true and original? "And if even you do see more than those who are not so fortunate and who have to remain at home," Davis surmises, "still you are so ignorant in comparison with those who have lived here for years and to whom the whole of Africa is a speculation in land or railroads" (Letter to Mother, March 11). What gives *him* the authority to define a place or situation for an audience expecting a semblance of journalistic facts, Davis appears to be asking, when there is always so much more to any one story—more than he could ever convey to his readers?

Ultimately, he declares, "I am a faker and I don't care and I proved it today by being photographed on a camel" (Letter to Mother, March 11). Because he succumbed to participation in a standard tourist activity, Davis believes himself to be no different than those other foreign travelers, unaware and uninformed in regard to the lands surrounding them. By deeming himself a "faker," the venerable reporter ostensibly critiques all American journalism, linking himself, and by extension the profession, to inauthenticity. Yet whatever moments of self-doubt Davis encountered, he managed to overcome and counteract them, inhabiting his role of "faker," or as I would amend it, his role of artificer. In his ability to change "costume" effortlessly, as John D. Seelye describes it, Davis could play "representative of high society" as well as "a man who could move with ease through dangerous environs, whether the slums of New York City or the jungles of Central America" (8). As a reporter and war correspondent, Davis intuited the costumes necessary and executed convincing performances, in both his public persona and his writing—and he relished the artifice of these endeavors.

During Davis's time, he was considered "the greatest recorder and reporter of things that he had seen of any man, perhaps, that ever lived" (Morris 5). In the 1890s, he captivated the nation's youth through his reporting, short stories, and even his Gibson Man countenance (see figure 2.1). The satirical adventure "The Reporter Who Made Himself King," published in Davis's *Stories for Boys* (1891), ruminates on the power of the newspaper and the reporter to manipulate society. The story's rhetorical use of *making news* aptly encompasses the mythology of the reporter that Davis himself engenders within youth culture near the turn of the nineteenth century. The act of writing necessarily *creates*; thus, the reporter "makes" news as he writes it, as opposed to simply functioning as a mirror of society. To this end, I see Davis using his stories that were for or featured young people as a means to respond to the dangers and empowering possibilities of artifice. Through his "cub reporter"–type characters, Davis invites young readers to participate in the process of artifice, one that includes empirical investigation as well as innovative storytelling. Both undermining and commending American journalism, Davis's characters show the artifice of the newspaper, and in doing so, show youth's ability to unsettle and reconfigure the news, literally and figuratively.

In reevaluating Davis's youth-centric stories through the lens of late-nineteenth-century journalism, we gain insight into how children's literature (and mainstream literature appreciated by children) grapples with news culture, and we see how it continues to operate as a means to challenge traditional power structures. Specifically, this chapter explores how the idea of "making news" and

Figure 2.1. Undated photograph of Richard Harding Davis. This photograph, probably taken in the late 1890s, shows Davis enjoying a new national amusement—bicycling. (Richard Harding Davis Collection, Albert and Shirley Small Special Collections Library, University of Virginia, Charlottesville).

the figure of the late-nineteenth-century reporter intersect with youth culture in Davis's "Gallegher: A Newspaper Story" and "The Reporter Who Made Himself King." Through focusing on the construct of journalistic news, these stories destabilize conventional notions of "truth" and instead value the truth of artifice. "Gallegher" and "The Reporter Who Made Himself King" react to the journalism of the late nineteenth century and its attempts to obfuscate artifice. Instead of obfuscation, these stories embrace artifice, thus suggesting the young person's facility to subvert, realign, or rebuild hegemonic social constructs. In these neglected writings exists the message, one heralded by youth, that identity, agency, and truth come with active participation in creative and social construction. For journalist Davis, truth exists within artifice.

Davis's self-appointed appellation of "faker" simultaneously suggests his awareness of the vocation's limits and his resolve to subvert and reinvent journalistic conventions. Much of his professional life was spent in the business of truth-telling, yet in Davis's short stories, particularly those centering on boys and young men, the text illustrates ambivalence and skepticism toward facts. Journalism-centric stories such as "Gallegher: A Newspaper Story" (which Theodore Roosevelt loved for its "power and originality" [Roosevelt 55]) and "The Reporter Who Made Himself King" focus on the creation of news, and in so doing, promote critical dismantling and reassessment of society. Or, more simply put, they challenge the child reader to challenge the world and its conventions. In "Gallegher," the protagonist, a street-smart newspaper office boy who "w[ears] perpetually on his face a happy and knowing smile, as if you and the world in general were impressing him as seriously as you thought you were" (2), nearly gets arrested while helping the sporting editor scoop the other newspapers in a story involving an underground boxing ring and the murder of a wealthy New York railroad lawyer. "The Reporter Who Made Himself King" depicts a very young reporter-turned-consul engineering an episode that almost turns into an international crisis. In the context of the days of the burgeoning newspaper industry and the professionalization of reporting, these stories articulate a productive skepticism about journalism's mission, application, and influence at the turn of the century.

History and literary criticism often overlook Davis, despite the popularity and acclaim he enjoyed during his lifetime. According to *Harper's Monthly* editor Henry Mills Alden, his stories exhibited "'the gift of a master'" (Davis, Undated Letter to Mother, 1890).[2] When Davis is remembered, it is either for his war correspondence during the Spanish-American War or for *Soldiers of Fortune* (1897), his novel set in a fictional South American republic.[3] But in the 1890s, Davis captivated the nation's youth. Booth Tarkington underscores

Davis's popularity, observing that "all ages read him," but Tarkington emphasizes Davis's influence on "young men and young women" in particular, those who "have turned to him ever since his precocious fame made him their idol" (27). When he died in 1916 at age fifty-two, many still viewed Davis as the embodiment of boyhood exuberance. His close friend, artist Charles Dana Gibson, used Davis as a model for his Gibson Man—a partner for the famed Gibson Girl—and remarked at Davis's death that "[h]is going out of this world seemed like a boy interrupted in a game he loved" (31). In the same vein, novelist Gouverneur Morris wrote, "[I]f R. H. D. had lived to be a hundred, he would never have grown old," playfully suggesting that "the name of his brother was Peter Pan" (3). Buoyed by his manner of grand performance, akin to something from a theater production, Richard Harding Davis played a significant role in late-nineteenth- and twentieth-century youth culture, a role generally disregarded in recent scholarship within history, literary, and childhood studies.

Davis's cult of personality arose from his ability to narrativize facts during a period when facts became more closely "identified with reporters" than ever before because of the job's growing professionalization (Schudson 63). And if "news was more or less 'invented' in the 1830s," says Michael Schudson, "the reporter was a social invention of the 1880s and 1890s" (65). Davis was also working during the era's shift to "new journalism." According to Karen Roggenkamp, one of the "underlying assumption[s]" of new journalism was "that newspapers should principally provide entertainment" (xiii). "[T]he *Sun*, the *World*, and the *Journal*, among other papers," writes Roggenkamp, "narrated the news with an eye toward character, plot, setting, dialogue, dramatic pacing, and other literary elements," which troubles the distinction between the significance of actual events and the artistic license of the reporter (or editor) (xiii). In pursuit of both journalistic truth and romantic ideal, Davis constructs an alternative reality for young readers where curiosity, bravery, and a sense of moral goodness prove more essential than explicit facts. For Davis, children's fiction and popular fiction focused on youth serve as a vehicle through which he can wrestle with the professional limitations of journalism and the political, empirical possibilities of artifice.

The tension between the responsibility of being a fact-bearer and the allure of creatively narrating personal travels surfaces in Davis's recognition of himself as a "faker," as well as his stories that interlink the newspaper world to that of young people. Of course, the compulsion to escape the constraints of facts and the writerly limits of the journalistic form invigorated American realism, a genre that arguably ascended from Rebecca Harding Davis's *Life in the Iron-Mills* (1861). But here, I am interested in the particular ways in which, through

Richard Harding Davis, we simultaneously find critique and celebration of the reporter through children's literature, or, perhaps more accurately, literature enjoyed by and featuring children, as many of Davis's stories had a crossover audience. In both his professional career and his fictional work, he projects the idea of the reporter as one who *participates* in and *propels* the story. During this period, there is no need to look further than Mark Twain, himself a newspaperman and writer of boyhood tales, to observe the desire for escape into the elasticity and wonder of childhood fancy. " 'The longing of my heart is a fairy portrait of myself,'" Twain said in a 1905 newspaper interview. "I want to be pretty; I want to eliminate facts and fill up the gap with charms" (qtd. in Shelden 125). Davis fills up said gap through imbuing the act of reporting with a performative, almost fantastic quality that definitively affects the resulting "facts." Consequently, Davis communicates to young readers not only an intimate bond between the ideals of youth and journalism, but their capability to help script American culture.

America, Romantic Childhood, and Davis

Over the course of the nineteenth century, the development of childhood as a significant period of the human experience changed the types of literature produced specifically for children and also how children were depicted. The shift to a more child-focused culture in the United States begins near the middle of the nineteenth century by means of the periodical press, to which Davis and his mother contributed. "Nothing reveals the emergence of childhood as a distinctive and protected period in the middle-class experience like the juvenile periodicals in the antebellum period," contends Gail Schmunk Murray (48). These periodicals "became a dependable source of instruction in the emerging middle-class value system" and allowed "[c]hildren [to] t[ake] great delight in reading about fictional characters like themselves" (Murray 48). Even so, Anne Scott MacLeod argues that, taken as a whole, American children's literature of the early nineteenth century avoided emphasis on curiosity and freethinking. Literature, including children's literature, functioned primarily to articulate and establish national values for the fledgling country. However, while early American children's literature was, according to Murray, "a conservative medium" used by adults to "shape morals, control information, model proper behavior, delineate gender roles, and reinforce class, race, and ethnic separation" (xvi), a shift occurs in the latter part of the nineteenth century as we move into what scholars call the Golden Age of children's literature.

The Golden Age, generally bookended by the publication of Lewis Carroll's *Alice's Adventures in Wonderland* (1865) and the outbreak of World War I, emerges as British and American authors focus more on story, craft, and imaginative play, and less on purely didactic purposes. American children's literature of the period continued to both endorse and reflect nationalistic ideals—such as Twain's "American boy ... strik[ing] out for himself"—so much so that popular American boys' books were "virtually unexportable" to England (Avery 9). The emergent trope of the American boy "strik[ing] out for himself" indicates an interest in communicating ideas of exploration, discovery, and self-reliance to children, an interest that differs from the themes of most early-nineteenth-century children's texts. In *Huck's Raft: A History of American Childhood* (2004), Steven Mintz uses the image of Twain's outcast protagonist and his river voyage to "encapsulat[e] the modern conception of childhood as a period of peril and freedom; an odyssey of psychological self-discovery and growth; a world apart, with its own values, culture, and psychology" (5). Mintz suggests that the debate surrounding the figure of Huck, with his "youthful resourcefulness" and "spirited rambunctiousness," works to expose American ambivalence in regard to childhood as we continue to indulge both its "popular fantasies and anxieties" (5). Such "resourcefulness" and "rambunctiousness"—keen precocity and curiosity—and how children exhibit them figure as the central crux in this ambivalence because of their potential for undermining authority. While Americans value "freedom" and "self-discovery," the question of how much autonomy children should be allowed continues to be a contentious matter. Nevertheless, scholars such as Janet Gray and Melissa Fowler discern a distinct change in the attitude of children's literature in the later decades of the nineteenth century. Gray and Fowler contend that "[t]he founding of *St. Nicholas: Scribner's Illustrated Magazine for Boys and Girls* in 1873 marked the ascendancy of the Romantic construction of childhood as a space of innocent playfulness, and a corresponding program for children's literature that replaced the direct moralizing of earlier children's literature with an emphasis on fun" (39).[4]

Davis begins writing stories for children's magazines after Twain's high-spirited, clever pair of Tom and Huck entered the cultural consciousness of American youth. Twain's characters perhaps anticipate the adventurous life of the young Davis that is reflected in his reporting. Tom Sawyer and his stories belong to the nineteenth-century tradition of boy books, and in particular the Bad Boy book, a genre generally considered to have started with Thomas Bailey Aldrich's *The Story of a Bad Boy* (1870). Kenneth B. Kidd writes that the genre "defined itself against advice writing and domestic fiction," and that a "sense of enterprise is expressed by all of the Bad Boy authors" (52). While Twain and others wrote *about* boys, that does not mean their audience was composed of *only* boys. Beverly Lyon Clark examines the popularity of *Tom Sawyer* and *Huckleberry Finn* and asserts that both were "highly popular" into the twentieth century. She references a 1923 poll that showed "*Tom Sawyer* was the fourth most circulated work of fiction in U.S. libraries" (78). Certainly, given this widespread readership, a mixed audience of boys, girls, and adults can be assumed. Twain's fiction and similar adventure tales call attention to the curiosity and inventiveness of young people—a detail that boys *and* girls may find appealing—and they often feature the kind of exhilarating exploits that the popular imagination equates with the reporter's life.

The conflation between news reporting, adventure, and childhood found in Davis's fiction can also been seen in the daily press of the period. A 1902 article from the *Augusta Chronicle* headlined "Do You Want to Be a Reporter?" speaks to this public interest in the profession, especially for children, by soliciting assignments from would-be journalists. "There are in every community a lot of people who want to be newspaper reporters," the piece states, later specifying, "This is the work for which so many untrained boys and girls imagine themselves specially qualified." (5). The *Chronicle* writer explains that this lifestyle is one of constant excitement, as the reporter's day may consist of a "political meeting, a drowning in the river, a marriage, a cutting scrape, a railroad accident, a proposed issue of bond, a court house sensation, a sermon, a horse race, a baseball game, a personal difficulty between prominent citizens about which he cannot afford to make any mistakes—any of these or all of them" (5). These events constitute the basic ingredients of the governing world. For a child, often denied access to important adult proceedings, the knowledge of such a vocation would probably prove seductive—the idea of a job that requires attendance at harrowing, socially significant, and possibly entertaining events. An imagined career in journalistic reporting rewards a child through its possibility of providing access, agency, and a voice that were previously restricted. A reporter, the *Chronicle* article suggests, not only witnesses events that are exciting, mysterious, and important, but also has a hand in bringing such happenings into existence through the reporter's obligation to "write, write, write" (5). During the late nineteenth and early twentieth centuries, the professionalization of reporting and the blossoming of imaginative children's literature, with its "emphasis on fun" (Gray and Fowler 39), collide in their explorations of artifice as a means to discover truth and autonomy.

For nearly his entire life, Davis blurred the boundaries between the realms of artifice and reality. In an 1871 diary entry, Rebecca Harding Davis detailed the growing amusement she found in her young son Richard, or "Hardy," who loved playing "circus" and "pantomime," and took pleasure in "gallop[ing] about," (1871 Undated Diary Pieces). "I never saw Hardy so animated or lively as he was to night [sic], full of life and feeling, telling about the circus and pantomime & [sic] imitating every memory," Rebecca writes (1871 Undated Diary Pieces). This enthusiastic mimicking of circus and pantomime performances led Davis to attempt to create his own stories. Rebecca calls "Master Hardy ... the most amusing of story-tellers" after he entertains her one afternoon with a rendition of "The Pantomime" (1871 Undated Diary Pieces).[5] But while Davis was encouraged to use his imagination to create story and performance, he shocks Rebecca when he confuses the distinction between deception in art and deception in retelling actual events. "Hardy gave us great distress today by telling an untruth," relates Rebecca in her diary. "I'd rather see him dead I think than a liar. But he is too young to know the differences between a lie and a 'story'" (1871 Undated Diary Pieces).

The indeterminate bounds of fictional and reportorial story, and the fluidity between truth, performance, and craft, come to define Davis's writing. Throughout his career, his journalism functions as a platform for a specific kind of truth-telling: not a reporting of untruths, but as Schudson describes it, "a documentary fiction—the facts would be there, but their point was as often to entertain as to inform" (64). Conversely, "Davis wrote fiction as a kind of documentary journalism" (Schudson 63). The hazy, overlapping quality of Davis's fiction and journalism points toward his skill at articulating the authenticity of artifice—perhaps part of the reason why Davis was so appealing to youth of his time. In "Gallegher" and "The Reporter Who Made Himself King," the young reportorial figures seemingly direct not only their individual adventures, but also social order.[6] Children could look to the physical person of Davis and his fabulous exploits to find legitimacy in the idea of the young, adventuresome newspaper reporter. And they could look to his stories for endorsements of youth's capacity to be change agents through the depictions of young people not just reporting, but openly and explicitly determining the news.

"Gallegher"

One of Davis's earliest successes articulates his frustration with the current journalism profession while also presenting a new reporter archetype through the figure of a child. "Gallegher: A Newspaper Story," published in *Scribner's Magazine* in 1890 and later in Davis's first book, *Gallegher and Other Stories* (1891), advocates a vision of the inventive, curious, and bold child through the eponymous protagonist, a newspaper office boy. But the text also comments on what a newspaper reporter should be, thus yoking the ideals of the child and the reporter. Ultimately, Gallegher becomes a surrogate reporter and must get a scoop involving murder and gambling to the newsroom before the paper goes to press. In this, the story stresses Davis's model of participatory journalism, suggesting how children and reporters significantly shape culture and society through active involvement. Here, the child is not the subject of "kitchy-kitchy-koo condescension" that Beverly Lyon Clark finds so deplorable in contemporary culture (5), nor is the child the "powerless objec[t] of adult discourse" that David Rudd describes (17). The reporter who manifests through Gallegher embodies a dual child-reporter model of quick wit and action, one who values the process of creating and crafting story. In documenting the reportorial process, "Gallegher" shows artifice at work and thus displays how children and youth can "make" news, or, in other words, disrupt and recode long-standing social belief systems or cultural dogma.

As a story originally published in the popular *Scribner's Magazine*, "Gallegher" enjoyed a large audience of all ages.[7] In an article reviewing the August 1890 issue of *Scribner's*, a writer for the *Christian Union* remarks, "We do not recall any magazines of recent times which has given us in one number so many bright and readable stories" as that of the August 1890 *Scribner's*. "If we were to select one for special mention," the reviewer writes, "it would be Mr. Davis's 'Gallegher,' a tale of newspaper and detective work" (Review 1—No Title 183). The story offered both identification and aspiration to child readers through young Gallegher's bravery, pluck, intellect, and independence, while simultaneously providing humor to adults by means of his precocity. The newsroom setting works as the great equalizer—an environment familiar to all because of newspaper culture's pervasiveness, yet one that provokes endless fascination regarding journalistic production and the reporting process.

Gallegher possesses both an Emersonian notion of intuition[8]—which the narrator reveals within the first few paragraphs by acknowledging the boy's "knowing smile" (2)—and an admirable curiosity to continually learn more. Since he comes from the tradition of city-wise ragamuffins, "[a]ll Gallegher knew had been learnt on the streets" (2). And though, while admittedly "not a very good school in itself," such an institution as the streets "turns out very knowing scholars," and Gallegher eagerly "attend[s] both morning and evening sessions" (2). His urban intuition, which contributes to his seeming at once "so very young and so very old" (3), combined with this readiness to acquire more knowledge, provide Gallegher with a reporter's skill set. So, while "[h]e could not tell you who the Pilgrim Fathers were, nor could he name the thirteen original States [sic]," the office boy "knew all the officers of the twenty-second police district by name, and he could distinguish the clang of a fire-engine's gong from that of a patrol wagon or an ambulance fully two blocks distant" (2). Gallegher is a student of Philadelphia and its everyday happenings, with a particular "love for that element of news generically classed as 'crime'" (4). He loves chasing and anticipating the action of the day, like any good beat reporter.

"Gallegher" scrutinizes journalism's artifice through focusing on the reporter-as-artificer and his process of acquiring and communicating news. During the 1890s and into the twentieth century, a time when the field of journalistic reporting became more professionalized, debate arose around whether reportorial skills could be taught and honed in journalism school, as Joseph Pulitzer advocated for years and finally achieved with the Columbia School of Journalism in 1912, or whether a general college education was sufficient preparation.[9] Charles A. Dana, editor of New York's *The Sun*, however, expressed the notion that boys like Gallegher make the best reporters. More important than academic pedigree, Dana said in an 1888 lecture at the Wisconsin Editorial Association, is overall curiosity and a devotion to journalism's mission. "If possible, he should be sent to college," Dana says. "[B]ut, what is most important, he should be sent to the school of practical life and of active and actual business" (15). For Dana, a keen interest in human interaction and an understanding of the newspaper industry cultivated from youth serve as the crucial factors. In an 1893 lecture at Union College, speaking on the subject of journalists, Dana told students

> The boys who begin at the bottom come out at the top.... these boys do not all start out with ... the best education; and I have known very distinguished authorities who doubted whether high education was of any great use to a journalist. Horace Greeley told me several times that the real newspaper man was the boy who had slept on newspapers and ate ink. (28)

Here, Dana and Greeley contribute to the mythos of the reporter life by framing it as a rags-to-respectability adventure in which young boys live in the news building, and thus also reinforce the relationship between the worlds of children and journalism. By suggesting that the child's physical being consists of newspaper ink, Dana conflates the child and the newspaper. Yet the newspaper proprietors stress the dominancy of the newspaper business, with the child being subservient to its hegemonic control; the newspaper, as the boy's sustenance and bed, functions as the definitive authority figure. Davis's story, meanwhile, complicates these power dynamics and debates of journalistic professionalism by means of his street urchin–protagonist's ability to outsmart and out-report the newspaper staff.

"Gallegher" obviates distinctions between fact and fancy, and in so doing emphasizes empathetic reporting and the idea of artifice as a social-change agent. As such, the story frames the presumably difficult life of the impoverished Gallegher as an adventure in which the boy circumvents traditional power structures (as opposed to focusing on his material hardships). The text romanticizes the facts of Gallegher's nonexistent home life in order to highlight the redemptive, rewarding potential of the reportorial investigation. Indeed, Gallegher uses his social position to his advantage, letting it serve as a means of disguise:

> Gallegher, while playing the part of a destitute orphan, kept his eyes open to what was going on around him so faithfully that the story he told of the treatment meted out to the real orphans was sufficient to rescue the unhappy little wretches from the individual who had them in charge, and to have the individual himself sent to jail. (5)

Again, Davis assumes the language of performance, assigning Gallegher to the "part" of orphan. From what we know in the story, Gallegher *is* an orphan, yet considers this merely a role that he can slip into to "ke[ep] his eyes open" and gain access to "the story" of the "real orphans." The distinction between Gallegher and "real orphans" raises questions concerning the merits of the designation "real," further undermining, or at least challenging, the ways in which journalism can represent reality. "Story" takes on multiple meanings here as well. In the context of "Gallegher," it is associated with a news article or piece of factual information; this is probably how Gallegher would employ the word given his work with the newspaper. But given Gallegher's "part," his "story" implies something theatrical performed for an audience of city officials. Notice the ambiguity of the language. The exact nature of the "treatment" that the orphans receive remains unclear. However, Gallegher's "story," or performance, "was sufficient" to punish the orphans' guardians. The focus in this passage falls on Gallegher's commitment to his "part" and his dedication to gleaning a general sense of the orphans' living conditions, rather than the exact facts of the situation. His reconnaissance rewarded him with "sufficient" intelligence for a convincing show. But even if we do not know the facts, we assume mistreatment. In this, we see Gallegher acting for social justice. Moreover, regardless of the scope of Gallegher's embellishments, he manages to destabilize the narrative of the adult "who had [the orphans] in charge," as well as that of the local authorities, through his (possibly exaggerated) "story."

Gallegher's aptitude for disrupting and rewriting cultural narrative results from both his active state of romanticized childhood wonder and his association with the newspaper. More than specialized training or an elite educational background, news reporting, as depicted in Davis's stories, requires an innate knowingness and curiosity. Davis connects these traits to the idealized child figure represented by Gallegher. The text, indeed, idealizes Gallegher as well as childhood. It affirms his overall being as extraordinary and implies that all children potentially harbor such extraordinariness. After Gallegher's own extraordinariness leads him to a suspected murderer, the sporting editor stands more in awe of young Gallegher himself than of the possibility of solving a crime that has garnered international press attention. "'My boy,'" the editor says to Gallegher, "'you are an infant phenomenon'" (17). The editor then tells Gallegher that if he [the editor] can get the facts and file the story that night, "'it will mean the $5000 reward and fame galore for you and the paper'" (17). In this moment, the text conflates childhood curiosity, adventure, financial reward, fame, *and* newspaper reporting. Gallegher's remarkable gumption steers him into the high-stakes exhilaration of chasing down a criminal, and in this circumstance, Gallegher is made a representative figure of the extraordinary child, the reporter, and the newspaper through his actions. Gallegher, to borrow from Greeley and Dana, "eats ink" by means of consuming and working amid newspaper culture, and in return he speaks its language and ideology. It is a part of him, suggesting that he can participate in its production.

The scene between Gallegher and the sporting editor also signals a critique of Davis's news-reporting contemporaries. Gallegher, the newspaper office boy who is presumably not responsible for scooping stories, runs "breathlessly" into the home of the relaxing sporting editor, Mr. Dwyer, after dogged pursuit of the murderer and the means to apprehend him. Given the urgency of the matter, he excitedly tells the editor "that he had located the murderer for whom the police of two continents were looking, and that he believed, in order to quiet the suspicions of the people with whom he was hiding, that he would be present at the fight that night" (16). However ready he may be to execute his plan of attack, Gallegher must deal with the passivity of the editor, who cannot keep up with the animated boy. ("'Now,'" the newspaper man says to Gallegher, "'go over all that again'" [16].) Gallegher then becomes especially frustrated seeing that Dwyer cares more about job details and financial concerns than about pursuing the story. Dwyer informs Gallegher that the boy has been let go from his position because of his recent truancy, which resulted from Gallegher's time with a local police detective, from whom Gallegher elicited helpful "suggestions and knowledge" (9). Apparently afraid that he will lose his job, or that Gallegher will lose the chance to recover his if Gallegher is permitted to go with him to the fight, or both, the sporting editor tells Gallegher he cannot go—a suggestion Gallegher mocks since the sporting editor does not know the site of the boxing match. But to Gallegher, the sporting editor's weighing of such banal matters as more important than reporting the news diminishes the editor's standing as a journalist. The boy "wondered how this man could value a week's salary against the excitement of seeing a noted criminal run down, and of getting the news to the paper, and to that one paper alone" (18). The text aligns itself with Gallegher, prompting the reader to question Dwyer's behavior. Thus, when "the sporting editor sank in Gallegher's estimation" (18), he sinks in ours as well, because he fails to meet the journalistic expectations outlined by the text.

In this exchange informing us of the sporting editor's diminished "estimation," the text condemns similar journalists of the early 1890s—those who put economic comfort and convenience above the requirements of reporting a good newspaper story, and those who have lost the general curiosity needed for such reporting. In an 1889 letter to his mother regarding a particular story he was covering, Davis acknowledges that "no one will read it" and "there is neither fame nor money in it," but the work itself "has been most interesting and absorbing" (Undated Letter to Mother, 1889). "Gallegher" censures reporters who lack inquisitiveness and who fail to find a way to make their work "interesting and absorbing." Indeed, as Gallegher and the sporting editor begin their pursuit, the sporting editor exhibits all the interest of a napping cat. Before heading out by cab, the "sporting editor got out to send his message to the *Press* office, and then lighting a cigar, and turning up the collar of his great-coat, curled up in the corner of the cab" (19). "Wake me when we get there, Gallegher" he bids, since "[h]e knew he had a long ride, and much rapid work before him, and he was preparing for the strain" (19). While he may look the part of reporter, with his cigar and "great-coat," Gallegher deems it a lousy disguise. The boy, whose "eyes shone with excitement" and who sat overwhelmed with "the awful joy of anticipation," believes "the idea of going to sleep" to be "almost criminal"; the sporting editor's inability to passionately involve himself is comparable to the behavior of the crooks in question, suggesting that both criminal activity and an ineffective press harm the public (19–20). His apathy, the story implies, leads to apathetic journalism and an apathetic readership.

Interestingly, Davis reacts to the nuances of the journalism industry while remaining seemingly aware that he contributes to its problems. He attacks the cadre of lazy, passive reporters embodied by Dwyer and then takes aim at journalists who seek celebrity. "'I am Mr. Dwyer, of the *Press*,'" Dwyer tells a detective. "'You've heard of me, perhaps. Well, there shouldn't be any difficulty in our making a deal should there?'" (21). By the time *Scribner's Magazine* published "Gallegher," Davis had already made his own name in the newspaper world, apart from his parents. An article reprinted in a January 31, 1891, edition of the *Jackson Daily Citizen* (Jackson, MI) provides a "Sketch of the Rise of Richard Harding Davis," helping to illuminate Schudson's claim that in the 1890s, "reporters were, for the first time, actors in the drama of the newspaper world" (65). The 1891 sketch sets up Davis as a charismatic, daring, and somewhat mysterious talent. More than an observer and chronicler of the news, Davis reads as a figure who creates news. In addition to being a seasoned reporter and *Harper's Weekly* editor, the "cunning," "dark complexioned young gentleman" described in the piece also plays piano and sings his own compositions ("Literary Light" 5). "Among other things," we are told, "he went to live for five or six weeks among the thieves of the Quaker City, and landed six burglars in Moyamensing [Prison in Philadelphia] besides writing some startling copy" ("Literary Light" 5). Davis, the modern Renaissance man who also sends criminals to jail, parodies reporters who revel in their modest fame through the Dwyer character, but his own public persona and the ways in which it affected his journalism invite criticism as well.

"Gallegher" offers Davis a means to communicate a reportorial paradigm through the avatar of the child. At this point, the story assumes the pace of an action-adventure tale, with Gallegher readying for the "race to Newspaper Row," which occurs after the police descend on the illegal match and apprehend the murderer, and after Dwyer gets the story (25). While awaiting the sporting event, located in an old barn miles outside Philadelphia, Gallegher "could not resist stepping into the ring, and after stamping the sawdust once or twice, as if to assure himself that he was really there, began dancing around it" (26). Gallegher, the idealized child, curious and romantic, continually indulges in moments of imaginative play and performance despite the levity of the situation, as we see when, before the fight begins, he pretends that he is the boxer in the ring commanding the audience. But he also uses this moment of fanciful play—"indulging in such a remarkable series of fistic maneuvers with an imaginary adversary" (26)—to help maintain his sense of wondrous delight in the fact "that he was really there." Gallegher remains interested, intrigued, engaged; he wants to take part in the development of what is about to happen. Meanwhile, the "unimaginative detective" assisting Dwyer "precipitately backed into the corner of the barn" (26). The detective, another adult figure responsible for uncovering and piecing together critical information, [10] fails according to the text's standards, because of his "unimaginative" nature and his passivity, like Dwyer's. Instead of hashing out multiple backup plans or further studying the scene before the crowd arrives, he retreats.

The twist in "Gallegher," however, enables its eponymous boy to *create* news, the artifice of which the story carefully documents. The police arrest Dwyer for attending the match, preventing him from getting the story back to the newspaper before deadline. But Gallegher manages to retrieve Dwyer's notes without the police noticing, and steals himself away on a horse-drawn wagon that was earlier secured for their quick escape. This signals Gallegher's entrance for his grand performance. The boy embarks on a mad dash to outrun both the authorities and the clock in an attempt to reach the newsroom before the newspaper goes to print. This scene further elevates Gallegher to a heroic position, because his singular, selfless mission is to get the story to press. When men overtake him after he arrives in the city, he refuses their attempts at obstruction and resorts to violence to accomplish his task, which the text renders as a justifiable consequence. Gallegher yells at the men, "Let me go, or I'll kill you. Do you hear me? I'll kill you," and then he strikes "savagely with his long whip at the faces of the men about the horse's head" (53). The staunch devotion Gallegher displays underscores the story's idealized qualities of child and reporter, yet Gallegher's behavior also reflects an awareness of the urgency of the situation. The irrevocable action of the newspaper going to print symbolically certifies its contents as truth. At the newspaper office, the editors and press foremen can wait no longer for Dwyer, and the story mines this moment for maximum suspense, prodding the anxiety of the reader. Knowing that the newspaper must get to press and without any word from Dwyer, the night editor grudgingly utters, "[W]e won't wait any longer. Go ahead" (56). But, after further buildup of suspense, Gallegher finally arrives just in time to stop the presses. The child engenders a rewrite of the historical record.

Gallegher, as a romanticized, timeless version of the child, scoffs at the minutiae and routine of adult life that distract from more vital adventures. Yet as a good child and likable character, he *generally* respects the organizing principles of society (law, morality, newspaper deadlines), but he will bend them for a higher purpose, moral or otherwise. While the dichotomy of newness and knowingness functions as the story's demarcating line between childhood and adulthood, Gallegher remains extraordinary because of his skill at straddling this line; he exudes both innocence and wisdom. By venerating this exceptional child, the text perpetuates his likeness as an archetype for the American child. But Gallegher also generates an archetypal reporter-figure because of his ability to both know and innocently play, to both reflect and create. Moreover, in its detail regarding the dubious and sometimes arbitrary machinations behind reporting and newspaper production, "Gallegher" underlines the newspaper's use of artifice. By recounting its protagonist's adventure of *making* the news, "Gallegher" disassembles the components required to present the daily depictions of American life, thus inviting readers to see and harness the power of artifice and self-driven investigation.

"The Reporter Who Made Himself King"

The animated determination of the child-reporter figure in "Gallegher" offers an ideal for the adult journalist while simultaneously suggesting that the very traits needed for reporting are those often lost in adulthood. In this, Davis configures the ideal reporter as a perpetual child or youth figure, and the ideal child as the perpetual reporter. But this is the *idealized* version—Davis often implied that he was aware of the profession's limitations, which probably contributed to his desire for fiction writing. Thus it is not surprising that the satirical adventure "The Reporter Who Made Himself King," published in Davis's *Stories for Boys* (1891), ruminates on the manipulative power of the newspaper and the reporter over society.[11][12] Whereas "Gallegher" shows a child uncorrupted by, or at least uninterested in, the power of media manipulation and the dangers of artifice, "The Reporter Who Made Himself King" broadcasts its theme in its title. The central character here is a young reporter who signs up for a governmental diplomatic position on a remote Pacific island. He then manages to manufacture a small-scale war. While Davis's story could be judged as poking lighthearted fun at the industry in which he was entrenched, it could also be read as a warning about the ways in which journalism employs its artifice. As a text for children, the story ultimately presents an America in which power belongs to youth, and in particular belongs to daring, intrepid, and resourceful (reporter-like) youth. "The Reporter Who Made Himself King" hinges on the plasticity of fact and, through the young reporter figure, youth's facility at modeling national narratives. The narrator opens by describing the typical young reporter and the conflicting theories regarding his training. The "Old Time Journalist," the narrator says, "will tell you the best kind of reporter is the one who works his way up," one with "no illusions" or "ignorant enthusiasms" (1). Meanwhile, the reporter of the new generation leaves the university, trained under "the idea that he is a Moulder of Public Opinion and that the Power of the Press is greater than the Power of Money" (2). Davis colors the text with his own experience as a reporter, expressing both a deep reverence for the profession and a tired cynicism. The young reporter, through spending long hours working his beat, studying the landscape of current events, and carefully maintaining his cadre of sources, has more knowledge and "experience" than the "doctor, or lawyer, or man about town," yet he probably receives less respect, recognition, and financial reward for his efforts (3). But the story's opening, with its comparison of the older, jaded journalist to the (initially) optimistic young reporter, establishes an exclusive relationship between the newspaper and youth's specific capability to shape national consciousness by maintaining that "other men do not venture even to think until they have read what he [the reporter] has written" (3). This weighty cultural influence—its advantage and dangers, and its distinct association with youth—permeates the entire text.

In Albert Gordon, "The Reporter Who Made Himself King" produces the superlative enigmatic protagonist—he who is young, but also more experienced, knowing, and curious than everyone he encounters. The Yale dropout begins his "picturesque and exciting career" in "reportorial work on one of the innumerable Greatest New York Dailies" at just eighteen (4, 3). Soon enough, he "had been to Presidential conventions in Chicago, revolutions in Hayti [sic], Indian outbreaks on the Plains, and midnight meetings of moonlighters in Tennessee ... and had contradicted the President, and borrowed matches from burglars," not unlike the journalistic activities of one Richard Harding Davis. After three years of the "exciting" reporter life, Gordon decides not "to work again unless as a war correspondent or as a novelist" (5). These two occupational scenarios, it seems, offer the same rewards as that of newspaper reporting but also include a certain amount of freedom, both professionally and creatively. The war correspondent, a position revered throughout the story and a term later synonymous with Davis, is seen here as a type of free-agent reporter; while under contract with a publication, he is understood as having more autonomy in his coverage and descriptions of the events of battle. The novelist, meanwhile, enjoys complete sovereignty in creating his semblance of truth through fictionalized story. For Gordon, a character whom the text both sides with and skewers, the stations of reporter, war correspondent, and novelist all satisfy the young man's quest for adventure and the "picturesque." Truth only exists as *he* experiences it through his creative acts and the work required to produce those creative acts. Whether that act is news production or fiction writing does not concern him.

However, a career as a war correspondent is a capricious undertaking. The text sarcastically mocks Gordon's desire for war so that he can be a correspondent, wryly explaining that the "only obstacle to his becoming a great war correspondent lay in the fact that there was no war" (5). Yet as a children's story marketed to boys, there exists an air of empathy with those who ceaselessly long for the next adventure. The text goes on, however, to subtly scoff at Gordon for his "read[ing] the papers every morning" for indications of "war clouds" and his eventual "disappointment" with "peace" when no war comes to fruition (5). Gordon soon finds an adventure on the tiny Pacific island of Opeki after agreeing to serve as secretary under the island's American consul, an ornamental post created for an old Civil War veteran. On Opeki, Gordon believes he can begin work on a novel and reasons that his old newspaper editor would "wire him if there was a war" (9).

The text circles around the implications of a younger generation replacing and reconstructing the world of an older generation, as seen in the opening description of the old journalist and the young reporter, and then again in Opeki. Once on the island, Gordon soon finds himself in the position of consul after Captain Travis, the Civil War veteran, sneaks away, discomforted by Opeki's remoteness. Gordon takes on the role with inspired vigor, managing to even appoint himself a secretary—a young man named Stedman from New Haven, Connecticut (presumably a fellow Yalie), who has been living on the island in the employ of a cable company. Stedman comes with two British army deserters, collectively called the Bradleys, who pretend to be Stedman's servants. Ostensibly, Gordon and Stedman, two fresh-faced, Ivy-League-educated idealists, represent the energy and creativity that youth introduce into traditional power structures, made all the more apparent by the uniforms of Yale football jerseys that Gordon gives the Bradleys to wear.[13] Indeed, while Gordon in many ways emerges from the story as an ambiguous character, old Travis unequivocally represents the cowardice and indolence of an authority figure shown to be fading and ineffective. His status as a Civil War veteran marks Travis not as honorable and respected, but as aged and out of touch. This is further emphasized by Travis's spineless retreat and the note he leaves Gordon, which warns him to "[l]ook out for that young man Stedman. He is too inventive" (21). The notion that Stedman "is too inventive," evidencing Travis's fear of that which is imaginative or innovative—that which will be created anew—additionally accentuates his cultural irrelevance.

Gordon himself shows keen interest in invention, though his skill set differs from Stedman's talents in technological and material construction. His ambition is still to be a "Moulder of Public Opinion," and as such, he determines to "transform Opeki into a powerful and beautiful city" in which people will "lay out streets, and build wharves, and drain the town properly, and light it," and in which he "will organize a navy and a standing army" (32). Gordon and the idea of youth that Davis perpetuates are invested in not only writing the news, but also *making* the news. When Gordon sets forth his plans for Opeki, Stedman replies, "You have me all stirred up, Gordon ... you seem so confident and bold, and you're not so much older than I am, either" (34). Stedman, in his assessment of Gordon and the reporter life, stands in for readers who regret or fear an adult life of desk jobs and boredom. He tells Gordon, "I have been sitting in an office ever since I left school, sending news over a wire or a cable, and you have been out in the world, gathering it" (34). Gordon, "smiling, and putting his arm around the other boy's shoulders," readily comforts Stedman by assuring him, "[N]ow ... we are going to make news ourselves" (34). The rhetorical play of *making news* aptly encompasses the mythology of the reporter that Davis engenders within youth culture. The act of writing necessarily *creates*, thus the reporter, in essence, "makes" news as he writes it.

As expected in a humorous satire, "truth" gets muddled. After Gordon and Stedman try to strengthen relations with the locals, the tribal king appoints Gordon as ruler. This leads to rashness, confusion, and gunfire with a German ship, which prompts Gordon to shout, "A great international war. And I am a war correspondent at last!" (67). The "three thousand words" that Gordon writes up describing the events to send through Stedman's cable service become further distorted as a result of the cable operator, who sees financial opportunity in the escalation of an international conflict. The situation—in its spectacular terms—reflects a shadowy distinction between reporting news and creating national narratives. The cable operator, like Gordon, manufactures an instance that seems plausible and probable given his familiarity with news stories of the day. Motivated by the possibility of the company's stock share increasing as a result of a war, the operator accelerates events that he thinks *could* happen, and he believes his cables will eventually be "substantiate[d]" by Gordon (84). Taken together, the actions resemble those of the reporter looking for adventure and the newspaper publisher looking for commercial gain. These manipulative, exploitative behaviors seem to echo an impetus coming from some corners of the American newspaper industry during the 1890s.[14]

Davis, the Cuban Conflict, and Journalism's Artifice

Years after Davis published "The Reporter Who Made Himself King," he observed the same kind of dangerous artifice alluded to in his short story occurring surreptitiously in the newspaper coverage of the Cuban conflict as the war between the United States and Spain brews, and as the New York dailies and other major metropolitan cities compete for readership in the early days of yellow journalism.[15] Davis's letters evidence newspaper publisher William Randolph Hearst's willingness to spend generously on foreign reporting, but the end to those means remains unclear. Davis, working as a correspondent for Hearst's *Journal* in January 1897, wrote to his mother often in regard to the sensationalistic and misleading actions of his fellow correspondents and officials, telling her, "Everyone I met was an Alarmist and that is polite for liar" (Letter to Mother, Jan. 16, 1897).[16] Davis's mode of journalism necessitated involvement; he could report events after he grasped them, often through participation. But Davis could not reconcile his idea of reporting, whether descriptive or participatory, with the reporting work he witnessed in Cuba. "This new journalism is beyond my finding out," he remarks after observing the behavior of various newspapers and correspondents. "It is not news that they want" (Letter to Mother, Jan. 4, 1897). He goes on to explain, "They send [Cuban military commander] Gomez a $2000 sword and medicine chests and a keg of rum, every correspondent takes him something and then the Journal publishes pictures of the sword" (Letter to Mother, Jan. 4, 1897). This version of "making the news," the notion that he playfully satirizes for children in "The Reporter Who Made Himself King," offends his romantic sensibilities, veering too far away from his belief in the truthful retelling of first-hand adventure.[17]

"The Reporter Who Made Himself King" suggests that truth does not come solely from the news, but also exists in the act of making the news, and in the act of openly embracing and creating artifice. While the text parodies the extent to which Gordon will go to have adventure and excitement in his life, it still communicates the allure of assuming active, inventive roles during youth. It also shows that such agency is rewarded. In his lifetime, Davis sees ideas from his writings taken more or less literally. Instead of signaling an abstract challenge for the young to participate and create, to reinvent artistic and cultural narratives, "making the news," as Davis experiences in Cuba, means misreading, misconstruing, and deceiving. The situation in Cuba, Davis writes, "is a terribly big problem, and most difficult to get the truth of"; he mentions that he is "growing to be the opposite of the alarmist whatever that is" (Letter to Mother, Jan. 16, 1897). "[Y]ou would think the picturesque and dramatic and exciting thing would be the one I would rather believe because I want to believe it, but I find that that is not so," Davis admits. He discerns the discontinuity between what is being reported, what he is told, and what he observes: "I see a great deal on both sides and I do not believe half I am told. As we used to say at college 'it is against history,' and it is against history for men to act as I am told they are acting here" (Letter to Mother, Jan. 16, 1897). Using common sense, a common understanding of humanity, and his years of reporting experience, Davis attempts to distinguish between the preconceived "dramatic" story and the real story—and discovers the difficulty in this endeavor, much like what occurred with his "faker" realization in Cairo.

Complicating the Cuban news coverage are the young reporters who probably took Davis as their model. In describing the distortion of facts to his mother, Davis specifically points out the haste and lack of perspicacity shown by the "yellow kid reporters."[18] To illustrate the issue to his mother, Davis recalls being shown individuals and families "huddled together around the fortified towns living in palm huts." "I know they have always lived in palm huts," Davis writes, but laments that "the yellow kid reporters don't know that or consider it," and then they "send off word that the condition of the people is terrible [sic] that [they] have only leaves to cover them—and it sounds very badly" (Letter to Mother, Jan. 16, 1897). Besides the matter of contextualization, Davis finds the newspapers printing completely false news from Cuba, including items with his name attached. *The Journal*, Davis contends, is publishing certain accounts so as to control the news.[19] Much like the manner in which the young cable operator waited for Gordon to "substantiate" what the operator had already reported as truth, Davis feels himself shoehorned into an uncomfortable, undesirable position, leaving him "queered." Not only does Davis dislike the spuriousness of *The Journal*'s actions, his letters suggest his outrage at losing his voice. Davis feels "queered" because he is no longer in control of his own story—and, perhaps, because he realizes that no reporter can be king (Letter to Mother, Jan. 24, 1897, from Siego de Avilla).

"Gallegher" and "The Reporter Who Made Himself King" illustrate Davis's experience within and knowledge of late-nineteenth-century reporting and the newspaper industry. But they also reveal the ways in which youth, adventure, performance, and narrative are intimately tied to news production and our understanding of American identity. The romantic reporter, embodied by Davis's persona and expressed by the figure of Gallegher, represents an ideal. But, as "The Reporter Who Would Be King" and Davis's letters from Cuba show, that ideal too easily becomes abused and distorted to suit the whims of youth, the economic interests of those in power, or both. Through displaying the inventive capability *and* the willful folly of youth, these stories laud the paragon of the romantic reporter while simultaneously acknowledging the need to understand how the reporter uses artifice.

Davis contributed to the discourse of youth through his "enormously popular" short stories and his reputation for being "the most brilliant of the young American writers"; a "capable, active, and brilliant observer"; and the "youngest successful man in the world" (London *Daily Mail* clipping, March 26, 1897; London *Daily Mail* clipping, Feb.1897; undated New York *World* clipping, circa 1895). In his letters from youth to adulthood, Davis crafted his life so as to resemble a great stage opera, casting himself as the principle actor (whether it be his restaging of *H.M.S. Pinafore*, his latest sporting event, or his role as college newspaper editor). Davis's early letters, his later published works, and his reporting career evidence a youth culture that values imagination, ingenuity, and artifice. Journalism functioned as Davis's channel for staging his adventure—to legitimize his self-narratives, an endeavor of artifice that he made to varying degrees in his reporting and that he wholly promoted in his stories featuring and read by children.

Through exploring the practices behind news-making, Davis's youth-centric stories ask readers to thoughtfully evaluate journalism and other forms of institutional knowledge. But Davis presents this challenge not to condemn artifice, but to condemn its camouflage. Artifice is inevitable—it must be part of any story. Davis advocates for artifice because it empowers. In detailing the artifice of the newspaper, Davis's stories challenge readers to discern and engineer their own artifice as they see fit. They stand as provocations for youth to confront and rewrite America. Through "Gallegher" and "The Reporter Who Made Himself King," Davis reports to young readers the basic fact that all we have is our artifice and our ability to "make" news, a fact that should be publicly broadcast again and again. Recalling Gouverneur Morris's remembrance of a cultural figure who could "never ... gro[w] old" (3), Davis stands as a prototype for an ideology that continues today through not only children's literature and popular culture, but also through journalism's mythos—that of curiosity. Davis's name may be little known in children's literature and childhood studies, but his legacy permeates our ideas about young people and journalists, that of the reporter as perpetual, curious child and of the child as continually curious reporter.

Chapter 3

A Spectacle of Girls

L. Frank Baum, Women Reporters, and the Man Behind the Curtain in Early Twentieth-Century America

L. Frank Baum had been composing and publishing *The Aberdeen Saturday Pioneer* newspaper in South Dakota for less than a month when small papers across the country began picking up an article from the New York *World* in February of 1890. The piece provided a biographical sketch of the girl reporter who had recently become a national fixation as she journeyed around the world in seventy-two days, besting Phileas Fogg, the fictional hero of Jules Verne's *Around the World in 80 Days* (1873).[1] "Free from affectation and loudness," the article says of one Nellie Bly, "she is popular with all who have known her, except the people she has made uncomfortable through the columns of the World" ("Story of Nellie Bly" 3). Later in the article, readers learn that before the *World* hired Bly, she went to the newspaper's office in 1887 and "asked the privilege of going in the balloon the World was then sending up at St. Louis," though "[t]his suggestion was not favorably received on account of [sic] hazardous nature of the undertaking" (3). However, despite the refusal Bly received from *World* publisher Joseph Pulitzer in regard to the hot-air balloon stunt, the popular imagination continues to conflate Bly's seventy-two-day international escapade with balloon travel even though she made her voyage mainly by train and steamer ship[2] (see figure 3.1).

Nearly ten years later, Baum introduced the world to a different girl who misses the opportunity to traverse great distances by balloon, thanks in part to the action of a different "great" and "powerful" man (45). "Come, Dorothy!" the Wizard of Oz shouts to the little girl who desperately wants to return to her Kansas home (291). "Hurry up, or the balloon will fly away," he warns (291). But Dorothy cannot find Toto, and when she does, it is too late. "Oz was holding out his hands to help her into the basket," but his feeble efforts prove unsuccessful (291). "Come back!" Dorothy yells at him, only to hear in reply, "I can't

Figure 3.1. The New York *World* newspaper advertises Nellie Bly's seventy-two-day trip around the world. (New York Public Library *Digital Gallery*).

come back, my dear... Good-bye!" (291). Though Dorothy loses her ride home with the Wizard, she later discovers that she possessed the ability to return to Kansas all along through the power of the silver shoes and that she never needed the help of the Wizard, just as Bly later secured an extraordinary trip around the world for herself (see figure 3.2).

With the creation of *The Wonderful Wizard of Oz* (1900), Baum did what he did best in his varied professional career, which included journalism, theater, and retail—he did spectacle, not unlike the reporting stunts performed by Bly and other women reporters of the yellow journalism era in the late nineteenth and early twentieth centuries. In *Oz* and throughout Baum's fiction, the contradictions, anxiety, and ambivalence faced by young women as they enter the public sphere manifest themselves—in strange and subversive ways in Baum's fantasy fiction, and by more conservative means in his other, more realistic girls' series fiction, such as the Aunt Jane's Nieces books. Baum made his name with the Oz series, but he also wrote popular realistic fiction specifically for adolescent girls, under the pseudonym Edith Van Dyne to associate the Baum name solely with fantasy (Rogers 136). As indicated in his contract with publishers Reilly and Britton in 1905, the Van Dyne books were meant to appeal to readers of Louisa May Alcott's *Little Women* and its sequels (Rogers 135). In analyzing Baum's writing for an adolescent girl readership in conjunction with the protofeminist potential of the Oz series, I find Baum's texts invested

Figure 3.2. Dorothy watches as the Wizard and her balloon-ride back to Kansas float away in W. W. Denslow's original illustration for *The Wonderful Wizard of Oz.*

in exploring the construction of gender ideology through both the magical and the domestic by means of deconstructing artifice, be it in a fantastical realm or a newspaper office. The drama of the American woman's changing world, in which the leading performers were often women reporters, appeared daily in American newspapers, and both the gender politics and newspaper politics of the period saturate Baum's children's fiction.

When explored through the lens of the newspaper industry, as well as women's move into the public sphere by way of outlets such as the newspaper, Baum's novels serve as a critical response to the ever-growing role and influence of journalism. In children's literature, Baum arrives at a locus where he can wholly indulge in artifice and extol not only the magic of artistic construction, but that of social ideology and our ability to manipulate it. Because of the modern cultural associations of imagination with youth, children's and young adult literature in particular welcome the spectacular and that which is outside accepted cultural norms. As such, the Oz and Van Dyne series investigate and report the possibilities of womanhood as reimagined and experienced by their young female protagonists.

One of the more popular of Baum's realistic series for girls began with *Aunt Jane's Nieces* (1906), which "in its day sold as well as the Oz books" (Rogers 137). The Aunt Jane's Nieces series follows the adventures of three cousins, who first learn of one another's existence after their rich, elderly aunt becomes ill and must decide what to do with her estate. The initial rivalry turns into a sisterhood, and the novels, according to their publisher, attempt to depict "rousing stories of the experiences and exploits of three real girls who do things" (*Aunt Jane's Nieces* 2). In a later story, *Aunt Jane's Nieces on Vacation* (1912), originally titled *Aunt Jane's Nieces in Journalism*, the girls start their own newspaper in a small northeastern country town (see figure 3.3). With the financial support of their wealthy uncle, the girls use journalism and newspaper production to appease their "natural impetuosity and eagerness to be up and doing" (Chapter Three, n. p.). The "philanthropic undertaking" of a daily newspaper, reasons the favored heroine Patsy, "would furnish us with no end of fun, even while we were benefitting our fellow man" (Chapter Three, n. p.). Besides the overriding storyline of establishing a newspaper in a rural community, the novel introduces mystery with an amnesiac young man's arrival in the small community, and offers scandal through riotous locals who disapprove of the newspaper. But the thematic thrust of *Aunt Jane's Nieces on Vacation* evinces itself in the rendering of upper-middle-class female protagonists who are "rousing," yet always upright, morally good, and supported by a male guardian. (Notably, this "man behind the curtain" plot device occurs in the Oz series as well as in the Van

Dyne girl-detective Bluebird Books series, which launched with *Mary Louise* [1916]). Baum's girls' series, whether fantastical or realistic, manage to challenge and reinforce domestic gender ideology of the early twentieth century by exploring the boundaries of women's roles and responsibilities in the public and private spheres.

The relationship between Baum's texts and the historical situation of journalism reveals the necessary negotiations that girls and women made with male authority, patriarchal ideology, and consumer capitalism so that they could forge a greater sense of cultural autonomy and identity. In this chapter, I specifically consider *Aunt Jane's Nieces on Vacation*, in addition to *The Wizard of Oz*, alongside

Figure 3.3 Aunt Jane's Nieces on Vacation cover artwork. Baum originally titled the 1912 novel *Aunt Jane's Nieces in Journalism*.

the history of women in journalism in the late nineteenth and early twentieth centuries to show how they inform and reflect one another through spectacle, as well as how the fictional girl characters and historical young female journalists function as reporters of artifice through their use of spectacle.[3] Here, I use *spectacle* as a specific kind of artifice that depends on public display. How does spectacle engage with or challenge cultural gender expectations in the spaces of the newspaper and children's fiction? Similar to how young women reporters and their newspaper publishers tested domestic and gender ideology through spectacle and stunt reporting, Baum's texts—through spectacle—erode the barriers between fantasy and reality and diversify the ways in which girls can imagine their roles in society.

Young women and girls in media positions at the end of the nineteenth century and beginning of the twentieth century became their own spectacle: They were lauded for their efforts, but these accolades came in part because their public professional work was such a new, novel phenomenon. Baum capitalized on the "spectacle" of girls at work, particularly those in newspapers. As I will show, Baum celebrates women in journalism while pulling back from completely endorsing their full agency. However, I still contend that the hope for young women provided by Baum's texts is an important marker. They reveal how the use of spectacle, when combined with the larger background of women's inroads into the public workforce, forged a cultural moment that advanced first-wave feminism's aims of gaining equality for women outside of the home.

Spectacle and Cultural Ideology

In Baum's novels and American journalism near the turn of the last century, there exist the machinations of the iconic image from the 1939 MGM film adaptation of *The Wizard of Oz*: the man behind the curtain, a male huckster employing various means of beguilement to sell his ideas to a potential audience. Baum's novel deflates the powerful wizard by depicting "a little old man, with a bald head and a wrinkled face" behind the "screen" (259). As seen in the relationship between Dorothy and the Wizard, in *Aunt Jane's Nieces on Vacation*, and in the story of American newspaperwomen and their employers (Bly and Pulitzer, for instance), the cultural work of the man-behind-the-screen demystifies spectacle through the repeated public display of female agency. (Some might contend that Baum himself acts as "man behind the screen" through his girl fiction published under the Edith Van Dyne name.) In other words, the idea of "real girls who do things" advertised by a patriarchal structure is used because of its extraordinariness; it is a sight to behold and is thus marketable.

Yet beholding the sight also works to ideologically normalize it. The theme of woman's role in society endures as an underlying current of Baum's work, and the woman reporter serves as a fulcrum for this theme in turn-of-the-century America. Spectacle seamlessly moves through both the routine display of newspaperwomen's work and Baum's girl-centric books, suggesting that the realms of the fantastic and those of the real are always one and the same. Baum's texts anchor themselves to the conceit of exposing and embracing the means by which spectacle can be produced.

During this overlapping Golden Age of American children's literature and journalism—an approximate period between the Civil War and the aftermath of World War I—I see children's literature directly and implicitly in conversation with the generic conventions, growing ubiquity, and sensationalism of this period's journalism in the same manner as that of American realism. Shelley Fisher Fishkin argues that the realist writers, including Mark Twain and Theodore Dreiser, sought to escape "the limits of conventional journalism as they knew it" and took issue with "the subjects that were excluded, the superficial, formulaic treatment of subjects that *were* discussed, the lack of connection to any time but the present, the extravagant claims to authoritativeness, the failure to challenge the reader to think for himself" (8). These criticisms, in the context of children's literature, help elucidate Baum's demystification of spectacle. Through jointly employing and unmasking the methods of his particular brand of artifice, Baum works to not only "challenge the reader to think for himself," but challenges the reader *to create* for himself or herself.

In its most general sense, spectacle arises from associations with sight. The way I primarily understand and use *spectacle* aligns with the *Oxford English Dictionary*'s entry, which defines it as "a specially prepared or arranged display of a more or less *public* nature (esp. one on a *large scale*), forming an impressive or interesting show or entertainment for those viewing it" (n. p.; emphasis added). Of course, the beauty of a term such as *spectacle* comes from its ambiguity, and the word carries different sets of cultural baggage depending on the theoretical or historical context. I see spectacle as a particular type of artifice, given its connection to human artistry and its connotations of deception. Indeed, Aristotle thought spectacle was the lowest component of classical tragedy because it depended on optics.[4] Spectacle is exaggerated artifice that relies on beguilement through visual as well as performative means. But again, what happens when the exposure of beguilement is part of the spectacle itself?

To further clarify, my use of the term *spectacle* derives partly from Stuart Culver's Marxist employment of the word in his seminal Oz article, "What Manikins Want: *The Wonderful Wizard of Oz* and *The Art of Decorating Dry*

Goods Windows" (*Representations*, 1988). Culver incorporates the concept of spectacle suggested by Max Horkheimer and Theodor W. Adorno, who understand spectacle as a device of capitalism, a "promissory note which, with its plots and staging ... draws on pleasure [and] is endlessly prolonged" (Horkheimer 139). This empty promise, Horkheimer and Adorno assert, "is actually all the spectacle consists of" (139). By foregrounding Baum's history in retail and his editorship of a journal for shop-window dressers, Culver argues that Baum—the fantasist—and ostensibly the powers of capitalism create spectacle to entice consumers, a group to which child readers, Dorothy, and shoppers could all belong. However, *Oz* conveys ambivalence about consumer capitalism by having Dorothy merely window-shop the spectacle of Oz. Ultimately, she refuses to metaphorically make a purchase, or stay in Oz. Culver reads Baum's fantasy and the shop window as "a stage for the performance of a specific drama of desire" (107) with the human-like manikin "mediat[ing] between consumer and commodity" (107). "[L]ike the Wizard of Oz," Culver writes, "the window dresser and the fantasist are at the mercy of their own representational machinery, while the shopper and the child perversely find themselves at home in front of the spectacle of the manikin's frustrated desire for closure" (113). Culver's discussion of "the window dresser and fantasist" behind spectacle illuminates the idea of Baum's interest in exploring the very orchestration of spectacle and celebrating its "representational machinery."

The element of spectacle has long been an important feature of the newspaper and journalism in general. Journalism scholar Norma Green reminds us that "news audiences"—those reading Pulitzer's *World* and small-town newspapers over a hundred years ago or those reading *The New York Times* on their smartphones today—"are attracted to the unusual, the bizarre, and the supernatural" (41). Green provides a sketch of the selling schemes used by William Randolph Hearst and Pulitzer, noting that Bly's trip around the world documented in *The World* "was such a novelty that newspapers devised a game for readers to clip and save as a way to relive the journey" (42)[5] (see figure 3.4). Hearst's "P. T. Barnum-like promotions reflected ... [his] childlike marvel in all things big and noisy," Green says (42). The newspapers of Pulitzer, Hearst, and other publishers "contributed to the spectacle of daily life" (Green 42). The association of "childlike marvel" with spectacle is useful in that it implies that spectacle is something particularly suited for youth, and particularly suited for children's literature. The linkage also pushes us to think about how the spectacles in popular children's literature speak to and comment on the spectacles of the newspaper in turn-of-the-century America, and how this correspondence, with

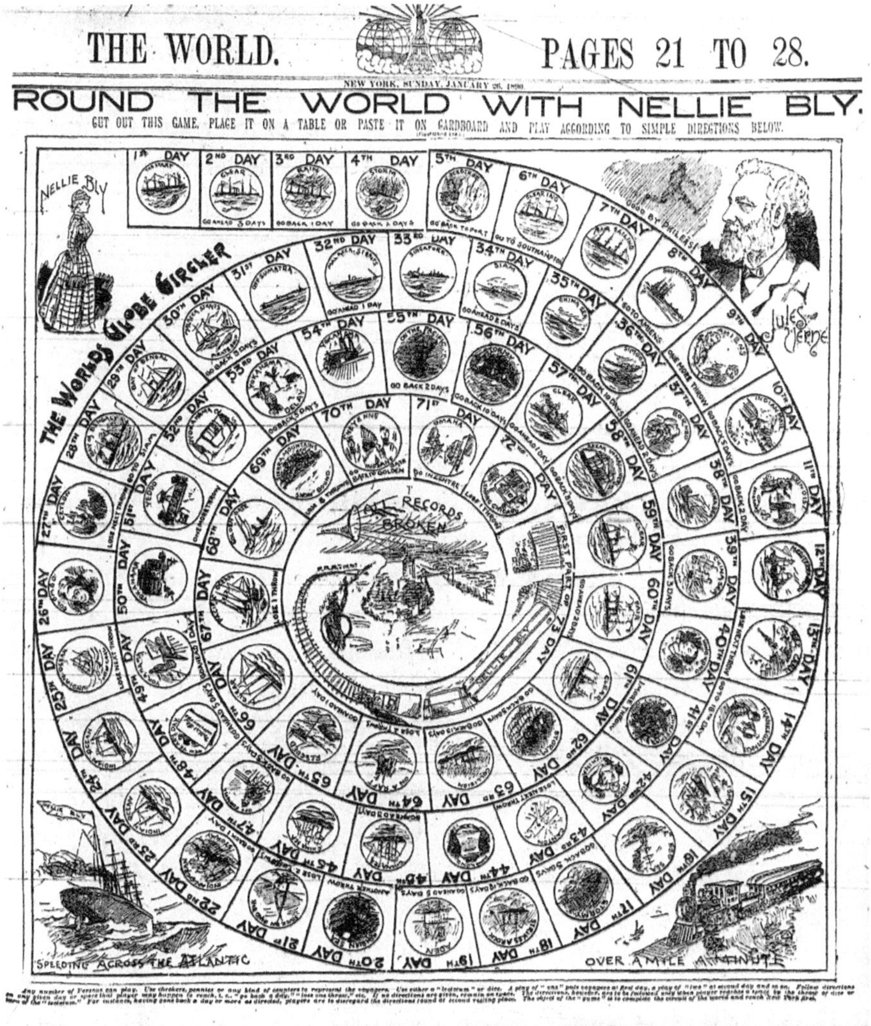

Figure 3.4. The *World* featured this board game during Nellie Bly's trip around the world in 1890. (Library of Congress)

its complex exchange of commerce and cultural ideology, influences national assumptions and conventions of gender.

Through its engagement with creative invention, Baum's fiction invites readers to uncover and reconstruct social and artistic realities. The repeated immersion into the episodic tales of the Oz and the Aunt Jane's Nieces series reinforces the myriad possibilities and nuances of American girlhood, both cultural and psychic. The conceit of spectacle underlines the required artfulness and artistry behind individual identity and social reality, and its use reminds girls of their capabilities to self-make as they see fit.

Baum, Oz, and Women's Rights

Newspaperman Baum absorbed the spectacle of Bly and other girl reporters near the turn of the century. Indeed, in both his fantasy and domestic novels, Baum uses a similar expression of spectacle to question traditional ideas and ideals of gender. The spectacle of Oz and its celebration of autonomous girls and women continues in Baum's Edith Van Dyne fiction aimed at an adolescent-girl audience, albeit presented in very different trappings. The girl readers of these books exist in the space between curious child and mature woman that Sally Mitchell has described as a "provisional free space" for the "new girl[s]" of the early twentieth century. Within this "free space," says Mitchell, "existed an imaginative and emotional power with fertile potential for nurturing girls' inner selves" (3). By intertwining ideas of spectacle with the "provisional free space" of female adolescence, Baum's texts both confront and appease early twentieth-century cultural assumptions about gender roles, inside and outside the home. The Oz series introduces readers to potentially radical ideas of gender. Consider, for instance, protagonist Tip in *The Marvelous Land of Oz* (1904), who is really a girl trapped in a boy's body. The novel's fantastical setting and generic classification allow it such liberties. Through the safe veil of fantasy, Baum can introduce events that might otherwise be considered outrageous. With the Aunt Jane's Nieces series, the text must work within a specific set of social parameters that allow for spectacle yet still uphold traditional girlhood prescriptives. Because many of his stories feature girl protagonists, Baum's fiction, whether set in domestic or magical realms, foregrounds the relationship between gender ideology and spectacle.

The Aunt Jane's Nieces series positions girls and young women as the ideal leaders—the moral backbone—of American culture and society. This comes with the caveat that the girls must be white, educated, and middle to upper class, and that they must operate, overtly or obliquely, under a patriarchal ideology. Girls can "do things"—that is, if they have a male benefactor to support them in their professional pursuits. Claudia Nelson asserts that American girl fiction reflects the complex relationship between its protagonists and the domestic space through "a focus on girls' conflicting desires for independence and for dependence, and an emphasis on the home as a source of both turmoil and power" (327). By and large, Nelson sees domesticity as "an overarching theme for the genre, which explores and models—sometimes conservatively, sometimes subversively—girls' aspirations within or away from the private sphere" (327). Ultimately, however, "[t]he heroes of boys' books *do*; the protagonists of domestic novels *are*" (330; emphasis original). Perhaps reacting to this predominant trope, Baum's publishers at Reilly and Britton inserted the introductory note to *Aunt Jane's Nieces* to emphatically stress that the girls in this particular story "*do* things" (*Aunt Jane's Nieces* 2; emphasis added). Though the Aunt Jane's Nieces texts cannot escape the hegemonic constraints of the period's inscribed beliefs pertaining to gender, class, and race, the books arguably strive for social change through small steps, advocating agency for upper-middle class white girls.

Given the influence that Baum's mother-in-law, suffragist Matilda Joslyn Gage, had on his life, Baum's biography all but forces a reading of the gender dynamics at play in his work. And certainly, the feminist movement of the second half of the twentieth century ushered in new, productive examinations of *Oz*. As Susan Rahn puts it, "To the feminists of the 1970s,... the 'girl power' so evident in Oz was one of its most attractive features ... a chance for children to think outside traditional gender roles" (xx). Through Gage, an outspoken crusader and leader of the National Woman Suffrage Association, Baum came into direct contact with the early feminist movement. The rhetoric of both Gage's *Women, Church and State* (1893) and Baum's *Oz* conflate women's rights with magic, figuratively and literally. As a means to communicate that women must toil with determination to change their social position, Gage chooses a fantastical rhetoric, declaring "power possessed consciously will give its possessor power to work magic" (234). This statement equates asserting one's voice, or "power possessed consciously," to wielding magic. In one sense, then, when women engage in the public sphere, as newspaperwomen did through their reporting and writing, they "work magic" and therefore create a kind of spectacle. For Gage, power and equality for women require spectacle.

The Oz books of Gage's son-in-law are populated by an empire of powerful, magical female sovereigns. *Oz* and its sequels illustrate a hyper-image of the actions Gage believed women must take up. For Gage, the church was the principal factor limiting women through its emphasis on ideas of supposed naturalness for men and women. She pays significant attention to the church's damnation of witchcraft and nonnatural women and the detrimental toll this took on women's ability to exercise and advocate for their rights, averring that "as soon as a system of religion was adopted which taught the greater sinfulness of women ... the persecution for witchcraft became chiefly directed against women" (226). Whereas the persecution of witches and subsequent propaganda against women who strayed from traditional religious dogma concerning gender roles effectively marginalized women over the course of history, Baum revises the witch figure in his fantasy. In Oz, witches are women with power that can be benevolent and constructive as well as wicked and destructive, as seen through the good witches of the North and South and the bad witches of the West and East. Meanwhile, the wonderful wizard is defrocked as a man possessing no magic at all.

Gage's criticism of the fallacy of woman's societal and cultural roles parallels Baum's subversive interrogation of the domestic space in *The Wonderful Wizard of Oz*, which readers first encounter in the novel's opening pages. Dorothy's Kansas home destabilizes the idealized domestic settings portrayed in sentimental ballads, such as John Howard Payne's "Home Sweet Home" (1823). Baum turns a farm, a space quintessentially green and fertile, into a "gray mass" inhabited by the "stern and solemn" Uncle Henry and the unsmiling, "thin and gaunt" Aunt Em, both of whom are also termed "gray," indistinguishable from the landscape (17–20). Home, as Baum depicts it, is a dystopia transferred onto Middle America. Orphaned in this gray state, Dorothy seems to be a stranger in a strange land. In contrast to Kansas, where her human caregivers barely utter a word and recoil from a little girl's giggles, in Oz speechless water "murmur[s]" to Dorothy (34). From the doorframe of the Kansas house, she would gaze out into a silent expanse of gray; from the same threshold, the land of Oz greets her with a riotous view of life and color. In sum, Dorothy leaves a colorless land where her familiar guardians rarely acknowledge her presence and enters one where inanimate matter readily accepts and welcomes her. Whereas little attention was directed her way in Kansas, in Oz all eyes focus a worshipping gaze on Dorothy, telling her on arrival, "You are welcome, most noble Sorceress, to the land of the Munchkins" (36). Yet Dorothy soon forgets the gratitude that initially overcomes her after her release from "liv[ing] so long on the dry, gray prairies," for shortly thereafter, Dorothy automatically, one might even say dogmatically, calls out for her unhomelike home (34). She seems to speak against her own instinctive affinity for Oz, choosing to overlook its bounty for the sake of returning to a familiar, yet inhospitable, place. From this moment, Dorothy never strays from her quest. Even as she makes friends, achieves fame, and frolics in a colorful world, she remains fixed on the idea that she must return home.

During his journalism career, Baum openly supported a reevaluation of the cult of domesticity. He once wrote in *The Aberdeen Saturday Pioneer* that women too often "sit with idly folded arms or listlessly dallying with fancy work" when they ought to pursue a "regular occupation" (quoted in Baum, *The Annotated Wizard of Oz* 13). Indeed, Baum condemned the practice of giving girls "namby-pamby books" to read in preparation for domestic roles while giving boys "adventure stories" ("What Children Want" 168). "The girls as eagerly demand and absorb the marvelous as their brothers," he affirms ("What Children Want" 168). Yet for all the subversive challenges *Oz* presents in regard to the home space, its interrogation of domesticity remains largely lost on readers; the 1939 film adaptation takes as its sincere thesis that "there's no place like home." To the popular imagination, *Oz* reinforces the construct of home. The title of the book, which effectively shifts focus from the girl protagonist to the sham male wizard, also complicates the text's perspective. The "man-behind-the-screen" exploits Dorothy in his demand that she risk her life and kill the witch so that he can maintain firmer control over Oz. Despite its liberating gender possibilities, *Oz*, its women rulers, and even Dorothy's capability to send herself home cannot escape the hegemony of patriarchy. However, the text heralds the opportunities for cultural change that lie within fantasy, invention, and artifice; it invites patriarchy's dismantling. These opportunities also present themselves in the journalistic work of women reporters, under a comparable veil of spectacle.

The Cultural Work of the Girl Reporter and the Newspaper

For American women of the late nineteenth and early twentieth centuries to be understood as contributors to and influencers of public life, they had to make themselves seen. The most effective vehicle for altering conservative domestic ideology was the newspaper. According to Alice Fahs, in the years around 1900, women reporters "wrote widely of new work opportunities for women, developed new newspaper genres such as advice columns and interviews, explored new living arrangements for women, advocated extensive travel, and covered and promoted women's political activism" and thus wrote "into being a far-flung new public world of women" (1). At the same time, some of these reporters, often barely out of their teens, became known for publicity stunts orchestrated by male newspaper editors and publishers. Such tactics, while contributing to a wider cultural notion of the American girl's investigative derring-do, were undermined by the exploitation by male authority for newspaper capital gain. Indeed, Jean Marie Lutes explains that while, in some aspects, women reporters of this period "qualify as professional pioneers ... they often appear to be looking backward instead of forward, clinging to tired nineteenth-century ideas about women's roles and ... willing to profit from the modern press's interest in their shock value" (1). Newspaperwomen, in pursuit of the chance to legitimate the value of their journalistic work, found themselves bound in a nexus of potential exploitation, opportunity, and agency.

In his scholarship on nineteenth-century journalist Kate Field, Gary Scharnhorst contends that contradiction largely defined the professional conditions for women working in the literary and journalistic marketplace.[6] Field "was repeatedly forced by the exigencies of the literary market to compromise her literary ambitions in order to earn a living and support her extended family" (Scharnhorst 194–95). Such compromises, whether stunt reporting or writing solely for "women's pages," proved critical in establishing women's voices within the public sphere, argues Fahs.[7] "Many [turn-of-the-century] newspaper women gained a measure of fame, themselves becoming subjects of public discussion," she writes. She further contends that "the principle of publication permeated newspaper women's lives" because "[n]ot only did they publish their own writings, but ... they themselves were published—made public" (18).

Thus, Nellie Bly's seventy-two-day trip effectively thrust the question of woman's societal role into public discourse through the pages of *The World*, whose upper management concocted marketing schemes to help maintain national interest in the story. Maurine H. Beasley and Sheila J. Gibbons call Bly's excursion "[o]ne of the greatest publicity stunts of all time," and state that "the trip was rooted in theatrical—not journalistic goals" (112). In other words, though her adventure challenged traditional thinking in regard to gender norms, Bly also served as a means for Pulitzer and *The World* to increase circulation and revenue through her fame, as Bly became "a national celebrity with clothes, games and toys named for her" (Beasley 112). Ostensibly contesting the foundational conceits of domestic ideology, "Pulitzer promoted [Bly] as a front-page heroine, personifying the independent American girl" (112). However, Bly simultaneously figured as a valuable market commodity—a pawn in a larger newspaper-publishing game controlled by men and their market interests through the *World*'s various promotional contests and reporting stunts.[8]

The World managed to depict Bly as both the "independent American girl"—Henry James's New Woman—and a Victorian lady. The biographical *World* sketch published on her return home from the international trek in 1890 ascribes the spectacle of "Nellie Bly" to one Elizabeth Cochrane. "Nellie

Bly" may be a globe-trotting, courageous, autonomous young woman, suggests the article, but in reality, Nellie is the reserved Elizabeth, who resides with her mother:

> Nellie Bly is known in private life as Miss Elizabeth Cochrane. She is an unmarried woman, 23 years of age. She lives quietly in an uptown flat with her widowed mother. The kind of work that she has done has made it necessary that she should know as few people as possible, and on that account her private life has been a very quiet one. ("Story of Nellie Bly" 3)

To assuage any anxiety concerning her very public life and work, the text here stresses Bly's "private" and "quiet" life with her "widowed mother." Bly's trip around the world and other investigative exposés (such as her 1887 undercover reporting series that was later published in full as *Ten Days in a Mad-House*) allow *The World* to flaunt Bly before its readership for her novelty and independence. At the same time, the paper tries to sanitize her for a mass reading audience. She may *seem* a public spectacle, *The World* implies, but in her private life, she conforms to conventional ideas of womanhood. However, through *The World* repeatedly capitalizing on and publishing Bly, and through Bly continually accomplishing these reporting feats, the idea of an independent woman in the professional world became more familiar. "With the help of Pulitzer and his new journalism," Karen Roggenkamp further explains, "[Bly] had participated in taking a point of imagination, acting upon it, and surpassing it on a very public stage" (46). In effect, via means of this knotty cultural and commercial interchange between imaginative spectacle and social reality, Pulitzer, Bly, and the newspaper contributed to diversifying models of American womanhood.

Well into the twentieth century, the stunts of the girl reporter continue to complicate any easy understanding of gender politics, particularly any easy understanding as interpreted though our contemporary ideas of feminism. For a 1917 prominently positioned article in *The Tacoma Times* (printed under the large headline "Service with a Smile Is Service the Patrons Like, Woman Reporter Learns"), a "woman reporter" tells readers that her editor tasked her with uncovering the working world of the waitress ("Service with a Smile" 2). She explains her assigned mission to "get a job as a waitress and find out what their work is like, and honest-to-goodness from-kitchen-to-table story of a waitress' [*sic*] experiences" ("Service with a Smile" 2). After trying her hand at serving restaurant customers, the unnamed "woman reporter" surmises that the waitress's "bit of social service" is important in a way that implicitly reinforces women's position in the home ("Service with a Smile" 2). An even more peculiar front-page article from a 1915 *Seattle Star*—"Girl Reporter

Plays 'Fly' to Expose Seattle 'Spider'"—sends a "girl reporter" out to unmask a fraud psychic, whom she discovers to be a "home-wrecker." The case could be made that this is another Dorothy revealing the illusory wizard, that by means of this sensationalized story, the girl reporter and the work of women is legitimized. However, in both the *Tacoma Times* and the *Seattle Star* articles, the acerbity of exploitation pervades the manner in which the newspapers publicize and deploy their women writers. (Additionally, the placement of the "Girl Reporter Plays 'Fly'" headline directly beneath the larger banner headline of "Butchers Family with an Ax" forces an unsavory image of the brutalization of the female body, as the word "Butchers" is right above the words "Girl Reporter.")

In the early days of the girl reporter, Baum picked up on and responded to the public's fascination with Bly in his "Our Landlady" column, which was published in *The Aberdeen Saturday Pioneer*. Baum historian Nancy Koupal describes the column as a combination of "satire, fantasy, broad comedy, and verse" used "to entertain and criticize his fellow Aberdonians" (7). In these articles, Baum "commented outrageously on the absurdities of human nature and, like other American authors, used local settings and characters to focus on the larger human conditions" (Koupal 7). A column from February 1890 entitled "She outdoes Nellie Bly and Makes a Trip around Aberdeen in 72 minutes and 6 seconds" integrates the excitement surrounding Bly's return to the states nearly a month earlier. Mrs. Bilkins, the column's titular landlady, has been running about town soliciting donations for "poor heathen wimmin in Africanistan" as part of a church effort to provide them with "hairpins" (30). Mrs. Bilkins proudly boasts about the speed of her trip around Aberdeen, proclaiming, "Why that 'ere bold female named Bly warn't a patch on the way as I had to flummox around this blessed afternoon!" (30). The column demonstrates how the spectacle of Bly's international stunt cemented her persona in public consciousness. (In addition to its satirical attacks on church society and the church's choice of fundraising activities, "Our Landlady" deals in problematic depictions of class, race, and rural life.) Society's awareness of Bly lends itself to familiarity, as evidenced in Mrs. Bilkins's comparison between herself and the "bold" reporter. As such, the girl reporter operates as more than just a writer of news or agent of spectacle. In embodying both, she becomes a cultural figure through whom women can read themselves and reevaluate their personal and professional situations.

Near the turn of the century, newspaperwomen and their ability to, as Gage would put it, "work magic" served to accustom employers and reading audiences to their presence, in addition to cultivating a female readership who wanted to participate more actively in the world outside their homes. The number of women working in journalism grew enormously in the last three decades of the nineteenth century. Alice Fahs relays that while "in 1870, only 35 women were recorded to be working as editors and reporters," by 1900 that number reached "2,193 women out of 30,098 total journalists" (17). The new century evinced paradoxical effects for the growing number of women reporters. The spectacular element of women reporting for newspapers helped establish their readership, but their gender combined with their stunt reporting seemingly estranged them professionally. "By the early twentieth century," observes Jean Marie Lutes, "the metropolitan newspaperwoman was one of the most recognizable popular images of the women writer in America" (2). Because of this, the newspaperwoman was "[m]ore likely than her male counterparts to be pictured along with her stories" (Lutes 2). And since she was "likely to inspire controversy by her physical presence at an event," Lutes likens the woman journalist to "a conspicuous anomaly, hard to ignore even by those who wished that she would go away" (2).

The rise in newspaperwomen predictably coincides with more girls and women reading the newspaper. An anonymous item published in 1892 in *The Topeka Weekly Capital* proclaims, "One of the facts that speaks well for Kansas homes is that the women and girls are as great readers if not greater than the men and boys" (13). The writer takes care to note that both women *and* girls are "great readers" of the newspaper (and stresses that "[t]his is not sweetening to commend ourselves, old fellow" but is just "Kansas fact") (13). The newspaper functions as an entry into public life for women and girls, according to the writer. "If anybody imagines this paper is made altogether for men he is awfully mistaken," she says, declaring that "[w]omen want the news of the world and they want the political news, too, as well as the editorial discussions" (13). She warns that any "man who imagines women take the paper up to read only the receipts for jam and cake and the latest fashions is very much mistaken" (13). Man "imagines" woman incorrectly in segregating her to the private home construct of "jam," "cake," and the "latest fashions." This is all to say that while newspaperwomen helped normalize ideas of equality through their repeated participation in public life and various forms of spectacle, female newspaper readers also contributed via their engagement with "political news" and "editorial discussions." Taken together, these actions underscore Gage's entreaty for women to take advantage of the more familiar idea of "power possessed consciously" as well as that of spectacular "magic" (234).

Aunt Jane's Nieces, Journalism, and Spectacle

While *Oz* may ultimately buttress patriarchal culture, it attempts to legitimize female agency and authority by means of fantastic spectacle, and also in laying bare the "magic" behind the Wizard's fantastic spectacle. Unsurprisingly, Baum's Aunt Jane's Nieces series shows an interest in promoting girls' autonomy similar to that of *Oz*. However, given its realistic setting in the rural Northeast, the series must deploy Baum's preferred tactic of spectacle in a different fashion. Instead of magical powers and marvelous oddities, the series relies on the spectacle of the girls "doing things" outside the home and engaging in activities traditionally associated with the professional world of men (*Aunt Jane's Nieces* 2). A glance at some of the titles within the series proves instructive: *Aunt Jane's Nieces Abroad* (1907), *Aunt Jane's Nieces at Work* (1909), *Aunt Jane's Nieces in Society* (1910), *Aunt Jane's Nieces on the Ranch* (1913), *Aunt Jane's Nieces Out West* (1914). With *Aunt Jane's Nieces on Vacation*, the text presents a distillation of the ideological exchange occurring in the early twentieth century between newspaperwomen's work and children's literature in regard to gender. The spectacle of three girls operating a small daily paper draws attention to young women's capabilities outside of domestic expectations and naturalizes the idea for the initially opposed townspeople. Through demystifying the spectacle of girl editors and detailing the "representational machinery" (Culver 113) involved in creating and publishing a newspaper, the text approaches a collaborative, pluralistic understanding of what constitutes news, social truth, and gender. Ultimately, however, the girls' summer spent running the newspaper is itself a type of Oz-ian fantasy, functioning as their playtime to dabble in journalism before handing the financial and editorial reins back over to male leadership.

Oz and *Aunt Jane's Nieces on Vacation*, when given closer analysis, offer a satirical reading of patriarchy. Though *Oz* feels more earnest in its tone and in its ability to suggest that Dorothy has more power than society might suppose, it also lends itself to the interpretation that Dorothy cannot escape domestic ideology in her desire to return to lifeless Kansas. But again, the text implicitly critiques the dominant cultural mindset, while acknowledging and offering alternative possibilities. (And, of course, readers see Dorothy return to Oz in later novels.) Instead of a magical world, *Aunt Jane's Nieces on Vacation* uses the press to comment on contemporary society and show the power of artifice—particularly the artifice of spectacle, which Baum understands to be its own type of magic.

The newspaper that the young women launch in *Aunt Jane's Nieces on Vacation* materializes after their Uncle John remarks that he misses his morning paper. Millville, the rural community where his country home is located, lacks any such convenience. After Uncle John expresses his longing for the newspaper, cousin Beth replies, "The paper? That's what that queer tramp at the Junction House asked for.... The first thought of even a hobo was for a morning paper. I wonder why men are such slaves to those gossipy things" (35–36). Practical Patsy, understanding the newspaper's significance to everyday life, will have none of this, and exclaims, "'Phoo! ... [W]e're all slaves to them. Show me a person who doesn't read the daily journals and keep abreast of the times and I'll show you a dummy" (36). Because Millville initially has no newspaper, the text labels its citizens as dummies and anoints the three young women as Millville's redeemers via their journalistic participation.[9]

The challenge in the novel is not *how* the girls will publish a newspaper, an expensive and work-intensive venture even for a small daily. The challenge proves to be *enlightening* the rural country townspeople (in addition to overcoming the sabotage attempts made by the unruly factory workers of a nearby paper mill). When asked just how such a feat will be accomplished, Patsy does not hesitate to respond, "[W]hy, it's easy enough.... We'll buy a press, hire a printer, and Beth and Louise will help me edit the paper" (38). She does not take into consideration the cost of such an endeavor, or the fact that they may not be qualified to compose a professional newspaper. In terms of expense, "That isn't the present question," Uncle John tells them. He is more concerned with whether or not the girls "want to be tied down to such a task" (39). Patsy, Louise, and Beth have the luxury of undertaking this task because of their extremely prosperous uncle. As far as their qualifications for operating a newspaper, their privileged status as Uncle John's nieces equips them for the job. Louise highlights their entitled position by adding, "I think we could turn out a very creditable paper—*for Millville*" (39, emphasis added). Indeed, the girls surmise that the "sleepy Millville folks" need "a bright, newsy metropolitan newspaper" (40). Uncle John, utterly charmed and confident in the abilities and enthusiasm of his nieces, cries out, "I scent [sic] a social revolution in the wilds of Chazy County" (40).

The novel not only suggests the power of journalism to effect "social revolution," but proposes that through the newspaper, adolescent girls and young women can transform American society. The idea presents a progressive, liberating concept for girl readers, but the idea has specific, restrictive parameters. Patsy asserts the necessity of their mission to bring news to Millville because "[t]he daily newspaper is an established factor in civilization," and thus, to move forward with the times, Millville must produce a newspaper. She then rationalizes that the "adage" of "'whatever man has done, man can do' ... applies equally to girls" (42). It should be pointed out that these "girls" must come from the proper racial and social class and must work within a capitalistic framework. Newspapers are textbooks for the masses, which educated, morally upright women *should* write, according to the novel.

Given his background in rural-newspaper publishing with the *Aberdeen Saturday Pioneer*, Baum recognized the social, commercial, and moral viability of journalism (which he, at times, employed recklessly, such as with his racist editorials ostensibly advocating Native American genocide, a subject on which Debbie Reese, educator and scholar of Native American children's literature, has so effectively written). As such, the novel advocates that rather than reflect the raw happenings of American society, the newspaper should present a perfected version of reality. The constructed reality offered through *Aunt Jane's Nieces on Vacation*—coupled with the constructed reality offered through the newspaper that the girls produce—presents a wondrous spectacle in its slippery navigation between social and moral didacticism, broad entertainment, and literary aspiration. The novel itself delights in depicting (and mocking) journalistic construction. For Baum, the newspaper is another device for spectacle, like the theater, the show window, or the children's novel. In Oz and the Aunt Jane's Nieces series, Baum upholds spectacle while simultaneously acknowledging the craft and process of its existence. The central plot of newspaper publishing enables *Aunt Jane's Nieces on Vacation* to promote spectacle as it concurrently deconstructs it. In doing so, Baum subtly intimates a connection between artistic invention and social construction.

As a mirror of "civilization," the *Millville Daily Tribune* must "reflec[t] the excitement of the entire world," Patsy tells her cousins (64). But Patsy's interpretation of what constitutes "civilization" and "excitement" render a funhouse mirror image of the rural community. Meanwhile, Beth must "edit and arrange" the sporting news of Millville in addition to the religious items. However, when it comes to "murders, crimes, and divorces" (64), Patsy, seemingly equating Millville citizens to the innocent children of Rousseauian philosophy, tells the girls that these items are "[a]ll barred. Nothing that sends a cold chill down your back will be allowed in our paper. These people are delightfully simple; we don't want to spoil them" (64). In her newfound role of managing editor, Patsy has precipitously developed an ethics of journalism practice: "You can't educate people by retailing crimes and scandals, and the *Millville Daily Tribune* is going to be as clean as a prayer book" (65). The verb "retail" sets up the newspaper foremost as a commercial vehicle. Rather than relying on salaciousness, Patsy wants her paper to deal in aspiration and morality. Instead of reporting strictly that which *is*, she prefers to print that which *could be*.

The commercial and creative possibility of the newspaper, as well as its wide social and cultural influence, make it a symbol for American initiative in *Aunt Jane's Nieces*. The first printing of the *Millville Daily Tribune* occurs close to Independence Day, thus equating the innovation of the modern newspaper with the establishment of the United States. The girls "remained at the office to see the birth of their enterprise" (105), a recurring conflation that equivocates biological childbirth to business venture. "The girl journalists," absorbed "in the birth of their fascinating enterprise," wait inside the newspaper office while outside Uncle John "gave an exhibition of fireworks" (105). The scene welds together artful construction and natural, biological process through the birth metaphor, and delivers it under a spectacle-filled firework sky. Evoking the hybrid natures of the scarecrow and the tin woodsman, the scene signals the inherent hybrid essence of America, a nation birthed and naturalized through its employment of artifice. Baum seems to recognize that if writers can author fantastic, fanciful fairy tales, society can similarly create new worlds that expand a previously fixed sense of reality. The text conveys that there are other roads, or will be roads in the near future, for young women to take besides those consisting solely of motherhood and domestic duties.

The novel assumes a peculiar attitude toward the nieces, as it both supports and ridicules them. As in *Oz*, the text's cagey tone results in an overriding ambivalence. While *Oz* questions the conception of home and the domestic space, here the text contrarily casts doubt on the girls' work outside that previously challenged space. The story's obvious fidelity lies with the nieces and their efforts, but it continually evinces a type of cultural anxiety about gender (in contrast with the overt derision of the lower class). Regardless of what Baum himself believes, his writing reflects a burgeoning societal challenge to the domestic space. Yet it also conveys the widespread resistance to that societal challenge. This tension reveals itself in the first *Millville Tribune* edition. The inaugural issue helps establish the *Tribune* as "a wonderful paper," thanks in part to the work of "the skillful Miss Briggs," a veteran newspaperwoman who handles the "telegraphic news of the world's doings" (104). Conversely, "the local news and 'literary page' were woefully amateurish and smacked of the schoolgirl editors who had prepared them" (104). Miss Briggs and serious, skilled professional women in the industry deserve praise, while the girls' presumptuousness regarding their journalistic abilities and stunt-like approach earns scorn. Yet the text still finds immense amusement in the audaciousness of the enterprise. Ultimately, the grand spectacle produces entertainment and probes societal gender conventions, however fleeting and limited, through exploring the idea that young women can *run* a newspaper as well as write for one.

Newspapers used the novelty of "schoolgirl editors" to their advantage in the early twentieth century, capitalizing on the spectacle and stunt of such a notion. In the process, however, these repeated spectacles helped establish acceptance of women's public participation, albeit an acceptance generally limited to middle- or upper-class white women. A headline in the May 21, 1910, edition of *The Morning Oregonian* (Portland, OR) informed readers of an apparently bold experiment happening at the state university: "Girls Edit Paper. Oregon University Co-Eds to Show Men Few Tricks" ("Girls Edit Paper" 6). In its linkage between "girls" and "tricks," the article immediately signals a wider social and cultural ideological ambivalence; "trick" connotes artfulness and intelligence, but at the same time it communicates silliness (and conveys sexual innuendo). On one hand, the headline is praising and buoyant, verifying that the work of these women—part of the "[f]eminine invasion of college journalistic field"—will be equal to or better than that of their male colleagues. On the other hand, they can only do this with their "tricks," signaling artificiality and unnaturalness ("Girls Edit Paper" 6). *The Morning Oregonian* and the college newspaper demonstrate why spectacle as political or commercial tactic proves problematic. Since spectacle is rooted in observation, it results in exposure; the *concept* of newspaperwomen (and working women in general) spreads throughout communities and becomes more accepted. But *the young women themselves* are also exposed and risk reinforcing and reifying patriarchal ideology.

The *Oregonian* tells of "Miss Helen Higbee," "one of the moving spirits in the feminine invasion of college newspaperdom," who will be the "city editor and sporting editor of the Women's Edition" ("Girls Edit Paper" 6). In describing the talent of Helen Higbee and describing the "masculines who hope to be 'written up'" by Helen, the newspaper positions her work as something largely for consumption by the college's male readership, and suggests that "the star reporter" is also an object to be had ("Girls Edit Paper" 6) (though some might argue that Helen is in the active role of "writing up"). Her journalism, then, can only be legitimized in terms of the male gaze. This, of course, points toward the gray area between exposure and exploitation, but should also remind us of the historical context enmeshed in the tenets of patriarchy—and the adeptness of turn-of-the-century newspapers and children's fiction in using spectacle as a means to revise those formerly unyielding tenets.

Two years after it published the article informing readers of the campus newspaper's "Women's Edition," *The Morning Oregonian* published another piece highlighting the work of women in journalism under the headline "Three Vancouver Girls Newspaper's Sole Staff" ("Three Vancouver Girls" 14). The

Washington city, according to the article, holds "[t]he distinction of having a daily and weekly newspaper written, edited, proofread and made up entirely by women" ("Three Vancouver Girls" 14). The account given of the "young women" both naturalizes their work and makes a spectacle of it ("Three Vancouver Girls" 14). The main reporter, Miss Bartow, "covers assignments as would a young man," suggesting that the expectation would be for a woman to report on stories differently than a man, and thus, that this woman reporter deviates from the norm ("Three Vancouver Girls" 14). But in recognizing that Miss Bartow works in the same manner as "a young man," the article also shows opportunities outside of constructed gender expectations. Indeed, Miss Bartow undertakes all the same anticipated male-reporter responsibilities that necessitate immersion into public life, and as such, she "attends meetings of the Commercial Club" and "visits the usual sources of news, including the undertakers' offices, and writes the stories" ("Three Vancouver Girls" 14).

The article consistently emphasizes the women's extraordinariness alongside their persistence, essentially "other"-ing them while also including them in a collective American ethos of industriousness. Readers learn that "[u]ntil they were told it is unusual for women to publish a paper without the assistance of a man," the three women "did not seem to think they were doing anything out of the ordinary. When an unpleasant task comes for them to perform, they merely go ahead and do it and that's all there is to it" ("Three Vancouver Girls" 14). Again, a sense of duality encompasses the text. The women will "go ahead" and do any task needed to ensure the paper's completion, indicating the ability and inclination for these women to undertake such actions. Yet the article declares that these women are "out of the ordinary"—indeed, that is the very premise for publishing a story about them. The overall effect, ultimately, serves to make the "out of the ordinary" seem more or less ordinary.

But the "Three Vancouver Girls" of the 1912 article do not own their newspaper. As such, another "man behind the screen," like Uncle John from *Aunt Jane's Nieces on Vacation* or *Oz*'s Wizard, aids in the operation of the "Three Vancouver Girls." "E. E. Beard is owner of the paper, but his presence is not required to have the paper go to press on time," the newspaper reports ("Three Vancouver Girls" 14). "He is frequently called away from the city, leaving the paper solely in the girls' charge, and they have not had any libel suits" ("Three Vancouver Girls" 14). Similar to the peripheral Uncle John or the evasive Wizard, Beard reinforces the hegemonic conceit that men control the success and continuation of the public professions while recognizing women's skilled competence, given the women journalists' ability to avoid legal and financial repercussions.

The shared discourse of spectacle and gender ideology between Baum's girl fiction and contemporaneous newspapers continues the conversation of the public woman and her role outside the home. *Aunt Jane's Nieces on Vacation* explicitly addresses this through the girls' involvement with a newspaper, although as mentioned, their time in the newspaper industry is akin to a kind of playtime or game of make-believe. But the novel does feature a young newspaper sketch artist from New York City earning a living from her journalism work. The character of Hetty troubles the novel's configuration of gender in suggesting that the fast-paced, vice-filled world of big-city newspapers forces the talented artist to "drink and dissipation" (96). The simple country life and an eventual marriage, in addition her important role at the *Millville Daily Tribune*, saves her from "perdition" (96). Like the exploitation of the female stunt reporter, Hetty presents the continued ambivalence surrounding newspaperwomen in the new century. In the same manner that the novel establishes a relationship of both reverence and scorn for newspapers and newspaperwomen, it likewise expresses ambiguity in regard to women's vulnerability in the public sphere.

When Hetty comes to the *Tribune* offices to start work with Patsy, Beth, and Louise, the text establishes a clear divide between the working-class newspaper girl and the upper-class nieces who look on Hetty "in undisguised astonishment" (93). Her initial disheveled appearance indicates the toll that New York City newspaper life has taken on her:

> Her face bore marks of considerable dissipation and there was a broad scar underneath her right eye. Her hair was thin.... The girl's dress was as queer and untidy as her personal appearance.... A round cap of the same material as her dress was set jauntily on the back of her head, and over her shoulder was slung a flat satchel of worn leather. There was little that was feminine and less that was attractive about the young woman, and Patsy eyed her with distinct disfavor. (93)

The novel's introduction of the newspaper sketch artist depicts her as losing any feminine qualities as a result of working on New York City newspaper. With her scarred, "untidy" face (suggesting involvement in a street fight or two), "round cap," "satchel," and "brown tailored coat," Hetty could be one of Alger's newsboys. Indeed, Hetty presents "queer" possibilities. This could be read subversively as promoting girls' or young women's ability to be traditionally masculine, but the text obviates such an interpretation by stressing heroine Patsy's "distinct disfavor" and Hetty's overall "dissipation." Young women "can do things" and should attempt to prove themselves in male-dominated professions, but Aunt Jane's nieces refuse to stray far from conventional appearances of femininity.

The text distinguishes Hetty from the nieces through her dress—inherently tied to her class—but also through grouping Hetty in a distinctive artistic category of journalist. "You're not real journalists, you know," Hetty tells Patsy, Louise, and Beth, and then reminds them, "you are only playing at journalism" (143). The sketch artist then defines "[t]he real journalist," a figure she notably characterizes as male (143). According to Hetty, the journalist "is a Bohemian; a font of cleverness running to waste; a reckless, tender-hearted, jolly, careless ne'er-do-well who works like a Trojan and plays like a child" (143). Because the journalist is a free spirit— "Bohemian"—he discards the traditional boundaries that divide professional and personal, work and play, filling him with passion as well as "reckless"-ness. The reporter "plays like a child," which in this context suggests spontaneity and intensity. "He lives at high tension, scintillates, burns his red fire without discrimination and is shortly extinguished," she further explains (143). Hetty puts herself in this journalist category, pronouncing to the three other girls, "You are not like that. You can't even sympathize with that sort of person. But I can, for I'm cut from a remnant of the same cloth" (143). Her description seemingly typifies an individual philosophy or psychology more than a profession, and the fervor attached to it communicates a specific veneration for the unconventionalism of "the real journalist." Hetty allows readers to encounter an alternative model of womanhood. Though her reporter lifestyle may be ostensibly framed as unladylike, it maintains a powerful romantic sensibility and attractiveness, particularly for sheltered adolescent girls.

It is not journalism itself that renders Hetty unfeminine, but big-city newspaper culture and the temptation that culture creates for alcoholic vice. Hetty's "talent and education" are soon established, as she comes with a recommendation from her former editor (116). Because he was worried about her drinking, he fired her and advised her to take the Millville job. Moreover, Uncle John's New York contact who initially hired Hetty told her that her employment with the newspaper could be extended if she exhibited "ladylike" behavior. Hetty's drinking is a problem, it would seem, not so much because of the consequences to her mental and physical health, but because it makes her too much like a man. Hetty tells the girls, "People get careless around the newspaper offices. They work under a constant nervous strain and find that drink steadies them" (116–17). Her story underlines the particular vulnerability of women employed in this environment. "I knew a girl, society editor of a big paper, who drew her five thousand a year, at one time," Hetty recounts

(117). Her anecdote continues: "She got the cocktail habit and a week or so ago I paid her fine for getting pinched while intoxicated. She was in rags and hadn't a red cent" (117).

The decline of Hetty and the society editor reflects the cultural anxiety surrounding the social and moral conduct of young women as they move into traditionally male-dominated workspaces such as the newsroom. The "cocktail habit" of male reporters and newspapermen is accepted because it "steadies" them amid their high-"strain" job, and because drinking is more socially acceptable for men. American women of the early twentieth century are still primarily associated with the purity and morality of the home sphere, and the text suggests that young women going to work in metropolitan newsrooms are especially susceptible to alcohol because of their innocence. Working in the most public of professions in the biggest city for spectacle and vice, Hetty's initial "dissipation" personifies an American fear of women leaving the domestic space.

One of the remarkable qualities of *Aunt Jane's Nieces on Vacation* is its very slipperiness—its overwhelming ambiguity in regard to the social and cultural codes for young women and girls. The figure of Hetty may be mocking the idea of women's vulnerability in big-city journalism, or it may be upholding her professional work, but either way, the text replicates it. The novel also carries as its banner the idea of "real girls do[ing] things," with Patsy explicitly declaring that women can do anything that men can do. Readers thus encounter a story that expresses the gender anxiety of its cultural moment, one rife with alarm and excitement in regard to the changing role of women. Baum exploits and capitalizes on this anxiety through relying on the spectacle of the young woman in public, which he continues to use with his girl detectives in the Bluebird Book series. In *Mary Louise*, for instance, an adolescent girl attempts to solve a mystery involving her family and is aided by the ingenuity of a female Secret Service agent. This spotlight publicizes and acquaints audiences with ideas outside of the everyday, which allows an evolution of thought. Such is the case for the initially resistant *Millville Daily Tribune* pressman, who exclaims, "By gum, folks, this 'ere paper's going to be a go! I didn't take no stock in it till now, but them fool gals seem to know their business, an' I'll back 'em to the last ditch!" (109). Indeed, such "gals" prove themselves to be good "business" for American proprietors of spectacle leading up to and following the dawn of the twentieth century.

Aunt Jane's Nieces on Vacation hints at the radical potential for young women, but does so in a safe, innocuous manner that ensures the novel's commercial viability. It presents the brief possibility of a new ideological landscape in regard to gender for its girl readers, but retreats back to support a patriarchal, capitalistic view of America. The pressman reminds us that the newspaper is first and foremost a "business," and, recalling Adorno and Horkheimer, depends on the fantastical and pleasurable elements of spectacle to further its capitalistic purpose. Spectacle also affects audiences because of its ephemerality, and near the end of the novel, Uncle John admits, "It was never intended to be a permanent thing, anyhow" (295). The *Tribune* temporarily allows Patsy, Louise, and Beth to "pla[y] at journalism," as Hetty says, creating commotion in Millville while demonstrating to readers the behind-the-screen mechanics of making a newspaper as well as normalizing the idea of girls working in journalism. The novel implies a discomfort in regard to women's roles in the newspaper business by emphasizing the temporariness of the nieces' time in journalism, and by handing over the newspaper to a young man at the story's conclusion. Moreover, through a convoluted storyline, this same mysterious man (who suffers from amnesia) falls in love with Hetty. Thus, Hetty's profession as a newspaper sketch artist becomes legitimized because she marries the new male publisher of the *Tribune*. Through the figure of Hetty and the idea of three young women running their own newspaper, the novel teases opportunities for young women outside the home and lets girl readers enjoy Mitchell's "provisional free space" before conforming back to acceptable gender standards. A man takes permanent control over the newspaper, Hetty becomes a wife, and Aunt Jane's nieces presumably move on to their next adventure.

Progress and Spectacular Construction

Literary and historical texts reveal that social progress and ideological change are generally messy, complicated enterprises. For American girls and women, these texts demonstrate significant compromise and indicate that reform requires a delicate dance between the familiar and the extraordinary. Indeed, Baum's fiction and the newspapers of his time suggest that cultural change only happens through the display of marvelous spectacle. The mediums of the newspaper and the children's story readily adapt to gimmick and novelty; however, they are both mediums that acquaint us with the world, and mediums that hold influence because of their ubiquity. The daily newspaper returns every day, while children's novels circulate among youth and are often read again and again. Spectacle introduces strange ideas into the everyday, but in its repeated use, spectacle acclimates these ideas to popular consciousness. Spectacle indeed helps inculcate the masses into the ideology of capitalism, but it also functions as a means of intrigue and exposure to ideas outside our recognizable social constructions.

Through Baum's unveiling of the man behind the screen, literally in *Oz* and figuratively in *Aunt Jane's Nieces on Vacation*, readers see not only spectacle, but the art of its construction. In this, readers gain access to the blueprint for a creative process. Through bearing witness to the machinery of spectacle in both fantasy and realistic fiction, readers—children—are offered a liberating concept: they create their own spectacle. Certainly, the nature of spectacle and its relation to capitalism force questions regarding the extent to which children's literature can escape the "man behind the screen" that controls them. (Indeed, Baum published his girl fiction under the pseudonym Edith Van Dyne to safeguard the Baum fantasy brand.) Also impossible to ignore is the very essence of children's literature in which adult writers must assume the disguise of a child, or at least an authority on childhood. But works of children's literature will always be in communication with and influenced by cultural ideologies masquerading as natural fact. Perhaps the task of children's literature lies with its ability to convey the fantasy of fact. At their best, then, children's literature and American girl books in particular provoke readers to ask, "Who is the man behind the screen?" and thereby interrogate the underpinnings of patriarchy around them. Baum's girl books allow for the magic of one spectacle to be exposed so that a more empowering one may be authored.

Chapter 4

Join the Club

African American Children's Literature, Social Change, and the *Chicago Defender Junior*

Marching-band drumbeats reverberate down King Drive in Chicago's Bronzeville neighborhood, providing the baseline for the medley of sounds that fill the air on this August afternoon. Families and friends bring out the barbecue and community spirit to watch the brightly clad high-steppers and other local groups of musicians and dancers move down the route of the eighty-fifth annual Bud Billiken Parade, "the oldest and largest African-American parade in the country" (Lewis n.p.). Thousands show up to see parade favorites such as the South Shore Drill Team and Jesse White Tumblers, a gymnastic-performance act founded in 1959 by White, the Illinois secretary of state (Black n.p.). Indeed, given the scope of this longtime Chicago event, leaders from government—both state and federal—also put in appearances. "A politician would have to be out of his mind not to be here," says Dick Durbin, United States senator for Illinois (Lewis n.p.). Incumbent Illinois governor Pat Quinn, ever mindful of the 2014 election only three months away, used the parade as an opportunity to stress the shared objectives between his campaign and the day's festivities: "We want to make sure that all of our children get the top-notch education they deserve, and that's really what Bud Billiken Parade is about" (Lewis n.p.).

Because of its history, the Bud Billiken Parade stands as family tradition for many area residents, and participation serves as a rite of passage. The grand marshal of the 2014 parade, singer Chaka Khan, fondly recalls routinely attending the parade during her childhood. "'I remember coming to this parade when I was a kid and my father used to hold me on his shoulders,'" Khan related to local news station WGN (Lewis n.p.). Speaking with the *Chicago Tribune*, parade attendee Yvonne Thompson explained that she "marched in the parade when she was a high school sophomore," and "[h]er daughter danced in the parade as a teen" (Black n.p.). This year, "her granddaughter became the third generation to participate" (Black n.p.). "There's a lot of history, a lot of knowledge and a lot of potential here," she tells the newspaper. Thompson further emphasizes the importance of the parade for community youth, stating, "Some kids are not motivated to do anything. The parade brings them out" (Black n.p.).

The parade's proudly displayed spectacle appropriately maintains a historical legacy that connects it both to the artifice of the newspaper and to children's literature. The Billiken Parade's ongoing aim to unite Chicago's African American youth and promote education stems from its original 1929 inception as an extension of the newspaper the *Chicago Defender* and its section for young people, the Defender Junior (Ottley 353). To "per[k] up" the waning newspaper feature, its editor, David W. Kellum, called on *Defender* publisher Robert Abbott, fellow *Defender* editor Lucius Harper, the national Negro Board, and Chicago's South Park Board to help establish the parade (Ottley 353; "Abbott-Sengstacke Family Papers" n.p.). Its primary mission, as described by the parade's first grand marshal, "'was to give underprivileged children, who are never seen or heard, a chance to be in the limelight for one day by wearing costumes, marching in a parade, and being seen'" (qtd. in Ottley 353). While the parade still survives as a symbol of perseverance, opportunity, and celebration for Chicago youth and the wider community, the newspaper feature from which it was derived has been largely forgotten. Yet during its early years, the Defender Junior not only gave voice to the black youth of Chicago, it also helped create a sense of identity for African American children across the country.

This chapter deviates from those preceding it in that it considers how actual children, as opposed to fictional depictions, act as cub reporters of artifice. Here, I argue that in the absence of a distinct or large body of literature for young African Americans, the Defender Junior—via the national dissemination and popularity of the *Chicago Defender*—functioned as an accessible space in which children and young adults could create, edit, and subvert cultural ideologies of black childhood. In essence, the newspaper became a form of children's literature, the exposed artifice of the newspaper enabling the creation of a community of and identity for black youth. As such, the youth contributors become cub reporters who uncover and endorse artifice's work. In its letters and contributions from child readers, the Defender Junior shows both the process of assembling creative artifice and the process of constructing social identity, itself a form of artifice. Through establishing a discourse representative of the lived experiences of African American children, the Defender Junior made manifest a sense of black children's community and identity for its readers across the United States.

This significant cultural work has been largely overlooked by scholars of children's literature and children's studies, journalism, and African American studies. But by examining it in the context of the development of African American children's literature and the rise of the black press, we see how the newspaper facilitated multiple developmental roles—social, cultural, creative, epistemological—for young people of color during the twentieth century's interwar period. The *Chicago Defender* and African American children used the artifice of the modern press to create a form of children's literature, further legitimating the experience of black childhood. In turn, this arguably helps spur the gradual proliferation of African American children's literature over the course of the twentieth century.

Because of the social and historical circumstances of black childhood, and given the fledgling state of African American children's literature during the early twentieth century, the relationship between journalism and African American children's literature took a different course than that of journalism and "traditional" American children's literature, which largely focuses on white, middle- and upper-class protagonists. Likewise, the African American newspaper also assumed a different course. The black press of the early twentieth century openly adopted a sociopolitical strategy and the label of "race papers" (Myrdal 908). The *Chicago Defender* championed its artifice and its agenda of social progress for African Americans, and in this, Defender Junior played a contributing role. The section (and the *Chicago Defender* as a whole) can be seen as a vehicle for African American children to uncover and engage with artifice to explore the parameters of race, citizenship, and childhood in America.

Through its collaborative process of construction and its acknowledgment of black youth's variety of experiences, the Defender Junior emphasizes to African American children their ability to create—artistically, intellectually, socially, and culturally. Because it values and lays bare its own artifice, the Defender Junior reveals how children's literature (as represented by the Defender Junior itself) can operate as an agent of change. My discussion of the Defender Junior articulates how it functions as both children's literature and change agent by means of interacting with and validating artifice through its cub reporters—its young contributors. I first consider the newspaper section within the context of African American children's literature before outlining the broader social history of the *Chicago Defender* in the early twentieth century, and then examine the children's section itself.

Introducing Bud Billiken

"Help Me Out, Please," implores the headline of a debuting column featured in the April 2, 1921, edition of the weekly *Chicago Defender*, the exceptionally influential African American newspaper circulated throughout the country ("Chicago Defender Junior: For Young Folks Help Me Out, Please" 5): "I am just breaking in on this newspaper game, and you will have to help me out" (5). He identifies himself as Bud Billiken, a reference to the small trinkets called Billikens, sold for good luck around Chicago at the time (5; Ottley 351). Bud explains that "[o]ur little doings get lost in the columns of this paper.... I don't like that. Do you?" (5), and he asks readers to send him their letters, stories, and poems so they can be published in the "Chicago Defender Junior" (5). Bud also solicits for news of anyone "planning on giving a little party soon" (5). This modest request for birthday-party happenings from African American children is consequential because it not only acknowledges a black children's community, but also validates this community's worth. The entreaty to send news to the *Defender* about their individual lives—and the possibility that these items will be printed in the newspaper—authenticates their being. They each have a voice, and others are listening (see figure 4.1).

While the genesis and contents of the Defender Junior may not seem radical or innovative in the context of our contemporary media landscape (particularly our social media landscape that enables youth to create myriad forms of community and self-expression), in 1921, African American children had few literary or textual resources that resonated with their cultural realities in positive or significant ways. And so when the Defender Junior featured an application to join the Bud Billiken Club and asked for additional reader contributions—an invitation to be part of an official group of young people recognized in print—the appeal must have proved powerfully alluring.

During the early twentieth century, few works were published specifically for African American children, and Michelle H. Martin explains that even the meaning of African American children's literature remains a site of contestation today. "Because of the turbulent history of African Americans and the power dynamics that remain in place within the American education system and publishing industry," Martin says, "the definition of this genre continues to be conflicted" ("African American" 11). Because scholars disagree on what constitutes African American children's literature and put different generic weight on the identity of the author and the intended audience, different texts receive the slippery designation of "first" African American children's book. Violet Harris notes that some "early writers and contemporary

Figure 4.1. Banner for the Chicago Defender Junior. The weekly *Chicago Defender* began publishing its children's section in 1921. (*Chicago Defender* 29 Apr 1922: 14. *ProQuest Historical Newspapers.*)

researchers" give credit to black writer A. E. Johnson and her religious-themed texts published in the 1890s (543). However, some occlude Johnson because "she chose not to portray African American experiences" (543–44). The work of Mary White Ovington, a founding member of the National Association for the Advancement of Colored People (NAACP), encounters the opposite challenge. Her novel *Hazel* (1913) presents a positive, though problematic, portrayal of an African American protagonist. But because Ovington was white, promoting *Hazel* as one of the early examples of African American literature presents inherent problems for scholars attempting to locate literature in which African Americans reclaim agency and express their historically subjugated cultural position. "Nonetheless," writes Harris, "Ovington attempted to provide African American children with truthful cultural images, entertain them, imbue them with racial pride, and inform them of the achievements of their race" (545).

Indeed, most scholars agree that a viable, representative literature for African American children first emerges only through the periodical press nearly two decades into the twentieth century. "[T]he most commonly accepted date for the beginning of African American children's literature is the 1920 *Brownies' Book*," Giselle Liza Anatol affirms, referring to the monthly magazine established by W. E. B. Du Bois and published by the NAACP as an extension of the organization's official publication, *The Crisis* (626). Martin similarly emphasizes the importance of *The Brownies' Book*'s two-year run, pointing out that before it existed, "children who wanted to read about black characters in children's literature could read about buffoons, mammies, Sambos, or savages, but not about the beauty of 'Children of the Sun' nor about adult African Americans who had consistently made positive contributions throughout American history" (*Brown Gold* 20).[1] Certainly, *The Brownies' Book* functioned as an influential precursor to the *Defender*'s Bud Billiken creation, and here I explore how the *Chicago Defender* children's section, capitalizing on the influence of the newspaper, took cues from and extended *The Brownies' Book* model to help legitimate African American childhood and establish a body of children's literature for African American youth.[2]

Despite *The Brownies' Book*'s ability to "present fictional and authentic models of successful Blacks (and in some cases, other minorities) who strive for identity and purpose without rejecting their own heritage and cultural values," the magazine's brief lifespan hints at its difficulty in reaching a larger audience (Vaughn-Robertson 496). Though Du Bois described the readership as an "unusually enthusiastic set of subscribers" who numbered approximately four thousand, the onset of "industrial depression following the war" forced the magazine to fold (qtd. in Pricola, n.p.), though the annual Children's Number continued in *The Crisis* through 1934 (Vaughn-Robertson 496). Courtney Vaughn-Robertson and Brenda Hill point to debate over the magazine's "elitist leanings" that probably exacerbated preexisting class tensions within the movement for racial equality (495). While children's literature for African Americans, beginning with *The Brownies' Book*, provided optimistic, alternative examples of black childhood, the uplift ideology that permeated these works remained a site of contestation within the black community (Smith xvi).[3] But in 1921, the *Chicago Defender* adapted and revised *The Brownies' Book* model for a mass audience. Sidestepping the implications of and anxiety surrounding uplift ideology, the *Defender* established a youth section built entirely on children's contributions and housed within arguably the most influential African American publication of its time, or any time since.

The *Chicago Defender*

During the Progressive Era and the Golden Age of the newspaper, the black press, particularly the *Chicago Defender*, intentionally employed the artifice of the newspaper to bring about change in American society. To understand the influence of the Defender Junior in shaping a sense of community and identity for black children in the early twentieth century, it is essential to understand the influence of the *Chicago Defender* itself, a news outlet still so revered by Chicagoans that former First Lady (and Chicago native) Michelle Obama wrote an exclusive commentary for the *Defender* website on the publication of her best-selling memoir *Becoming* (2018). Launched in 1905 by Robert Abbott, the weekly newspaper eventually became the "most widely read newspaper in the black South," and therefore "afforded thousands of prospective migrants glimpses of an exciting city with a vibrant and assertive black community" (Grossman 4). Abbott's biographer Roi Ottley contends in his 1955 study of the publisher that "with the exception of the Bible, no publication was more influential among the Negro masses" during the first half of the century (8). Sociologist (and the first black president of Fisk University) Charles S. Johnson once described the newspaper as "'one of the most potent factors in a phenomenal hegira that began to change the character and pattern of race relations in the United States'" (qtd. in Ottley 9). The paper struggled in its early years, but it gained readership after Abbott adopted an "uncompromising racial idealism, a policy pursued with such vigor that the man was excoriated as a 'yellow journalist' in the Hearst tradition" (Ottley 2). That is, Abbott proudly relished the role of artificer in ways that mainstream publishers also did, but Abbott did so in a much more open and blatant manner.

The *Chicago Defender* candidly tapped into the creative and social power of artifice to craft a new racial ideology.[4] Deploying an attitude of "unapologetic black pride, dignity, and assertiveness," Abbott's newspaper "waged a militant campaign against white southerners, fulfilling its role as the defender of black America against 'the crafty paleface' of the South" (Grossman 75, 78).[5] For this reason, scholars and writers give the newspaper credit for helping incite the Great Migration, a movement beginning in approximately 1916 that saw thousands of African Americans leave their rural southern homes for northern urban areas.[6] Ottley states that the number of black residents in Chicago increased from "40,000 to nearly 150,000 within a short space of a few years" (161). The national distribution of the *Defender*, its forthright, sensational tone,[7] and its specialized appeal to black Americans and their social circumstances helped unite a segment of citizens previously disconnected from one another by their exclusion from written and national discourse.

Across the country, the delivery of the *Chicago Defender* each Saturday became an anticipated occasion for many African Americans because it presented the possibility for a new national vision. "By 1916," says James R. Grossman, "the *Defender* seemed to be everywhere," including the important social centers of the church and the barber shop (79). Grossman relates the account of a "New Orleans woman [who] explained that she 'had rather read it then [sic] to eat when Saturday comes, it is my heart's delight'" (80). Circulation numbers do not accurately reflect the reach of the *Defender* since copies were shared between friends and family members, and issues were read aloud and "passed by word of mouth" (Myrdal 909). According to Grossman, the newspaper's sales in the early 1920s were between 160,000 and 250,000, though these figures may be overstated (79).

In an oral history recorded in 1972 for the University of Southern Mississippi's Center for Oral History and Cultural Heritage, R. Jess Brown, a lawyer from Jackson, Mississippi, describes the pivotal role the *Defender* and other African American newspapers played in his life from an early age because they showed both the violent severity of conditions for black Americans but also the potential for social change. "When I was a kid [approximately the 1920s], I used to sell papers," Brown recalls (Oral History with Mr. R. Jess Brown 7). "I had a paper route in the morning, and then on Saturdays I handled a number of black weekly papers, like the *Chicago Defender*, *Pittsburgh Courier*, and *Oklahoma City Black Dispatch*" (7). Brown explains that the *Defender* educated him on the racial situation of the South, particularly the lynching of African Americans by white Americans. The *Defender* did not shy away from depicting the brutality of these incidents and published photographs of these violent attacks. Brown says that seeing these images during his childhood "sort of stimulated me all along" (7). Brown's account implies that African American children turned to the *Defender* not only for the specifically youth-oriented Defender Junior, but also to ascertain the situation of black America and further piece together their cultural and social identities. Through the 1930s and the following decades, the *Defender* remained crucial in informing black southerners of national and global news, often inspiring them to become involved with larger social issues. On this point, in a 2002 oral history Reverend Harry Charles Tartt recollected, "When I was on the Coast, somebody was distributing the *Chicago Defender*. And that's how I found out what was going on in the rest of the world" ("Oral History with Reverend Harry Charles Tartt" 182). For black youth growing up post-Reconstruction in the twentieth century, the *Defender* revealed what it meant to be black in America, and through engaging with artifice, showed that this idea of blackness could be altered. The newspaper rendered the facts of American culture malleable. Specifically, through stressing the creative, critical role of its readers, the Defender Junior conveyed to black children their ability to make new meanings for themselves.

Bud Billiken and His Club

The influence and social import of the *Chicago Defender* among African Americans during the early twentieth century familiarized black youth with critical issues affecting their communities, but it also gave them a space to write, reinvent, and legitimize their identities through its Defender Junior section. The newspaper enabled them to symbolically report new truths regarding the signified of the signifier "childhood" through their personal stories of the black youth experience. For an article commemorating the seventieth anniversary of the *Chicago Defender* in 1975, reporter Odessa McClary details the newspaper's importance during her youth in the 1930s and 1940s. From a very early age,

McClary says, "you knew when Saturday came in my home town. Saturday was the day your mother and the neighbors set their money aside so they could pay that Defender paper boy" (56). Most pointedly, she highlights the lead player for her in this production—Bud Billiken and the Defender Junior. She writes that "the main thing in the Defender was the Bud Billiken Page" and that with "five kids in the family there was many a tussle and long discussion over just who would get the coupon to apply for Billiken membership" (56). But McClary goes on to explain that the coupon and application were more or less superfluous because of the community created through the reading and writing of the section. For McClary and others, the *Defender*'s youth page indeed joined black children together, but it also showed them the breadth of childhood experiences among African Americans. Each week, the section gifted them with "letters from kids living in places far away" who "described such interesting activities" (McClary 56). Additionally, "[t]here were drawings" and "even poems written by kids," and she remarks that she "learned a lot of stuff reading that Billiken Page" (56). In discovering the range of talents and worldviews among

JOIN THE BUD BILLIKEN CLUB

Every boy and girl reader of this column is eligible for membership. Costs nothing to join—you pay no dues. Fill out and return the application blank today and become a member.

Application Blank for Membership

Bud Billiken Club

I wish to become a member of The Chicago Defender's Bud Billiken club

My name is.................................

Address...................... Age....

City.................... State........

Parents' name........................

Figure 4.2. Bud Billiken Club membership form. A club membership form could be found in each edition of the Defender Junior. (*Chicago Defender* 29 Apr 1922: 14. *ProQuest Historical Newspapers.*)

young persons of their race, child readers secured a communal space of possibility that was public yet private, as "grownups didn't even look at that page" (McClary 56)[8] (see figure 4.2).

From its inception in 1921,[9] the Defender Junior defined itself as a specific, special space for young African Americans to learn about and engage with other children, as well as a venue to publish writing and poetry. According to Lucius C. Harper, a *Defender* editor credited with the section's creation, the Defender Junior became the "first time in Negro journalism" for "a column devoted to the interest of children" (6). At that time, the *Defender* "printed no comics ... and the Negro newspaper had nothing to interest a person from the ages of eight to fifteen" (Harper 1). Using his childhood nickname and the term for a popular good-luck trinket, Harper created the section's mascot and child-editor persona. Harper picked the original Bud Billiken from a group of *Defender* newsboys, "a quiet, sad-eyed, soft-spoken and well-mannered little fellow about ten years old" named Willard Motley (6). For the after-school position of Bud Billiken editor, Motley and Harper agreed on a weekly salary of $3 (6). Harper "made a photo of him wearing green-eyeshade with pencil behind ear," and Motly "wrote 'editorials' in kid fashion and appeal and answered letters from children" (6). Thus, while the *Defender*'s editorial department exercised some oversight, the composition of the Defender Junior relied almost entirely on the voices of young people.

Typically, an edition of the Defender Junior would be introduced by a message from Bud Billiken that described any news regarding the section and encouraged readers to submit letters, creative writing, membership applications, and any news of interest. These prefaces established the fictitious Bud Billiken character as a facilitator for the page and its readership, but they also enabled him to reinforce the idea that *the readership* created this community through *creating the section itself*. The application and membership, then, function as a means to "officially" recognize black youth identity. But as Odessa McClary indicates, the routine reading of the weekly Defender Junior proved to be the primary criterion for feeling included in this "club" of African American children. Part of this spirit of inclusiveness results from the rhetoric of Bud's introductory comments, which evoke sentiments of solidarity and collaboration. "The Billikin Club is going better every issue, and I wonder if you feel good about it," Bud says to readers in column published on Feb. 4, 1922 ("The Defender Junior," Feb. 4, 1922, A2). This opening sentence tells readers and contributors—the club members—that their words matter, and they share responsibility in the section's success. "This club and paper is edited by the young people entirely," Bud reiterates, "and you should feel proud to look at your own work in print" (A2). Their "work in print" stands as material evidence of childhood experience outside that of middle-class white childhood; once "in print" through the Defender Junior, black children can see themselves as an important creative, contributing community. Bud emphasizes, "It is our own production, Billikens all, remember," implying that the processes of artifice cannot be separated from the identity and community of those writing; the Billikens are writing black youth identity through their collaboratively constructed "production."

The specific self-portraits that the readers and writers of the Defender Junior provide destabilizes any one notion of what it is to be an African American child in the 1920s. The community formed by Billiken readers and club members reflects geographic and socioeconomic heterogeneity, countering any monolithic configuration of black childhood. The hometowns provided by contributors alone indicate the broad, diverse readership of the *Defender* in the 1920s. As expected, letters come from readers in Chicago and Illinois, but also Missouri, Texas, Mississippi, Louisiana, Nebraska, Georgia, Michigan, Wyoming, Colorado, and New Jersey, among others, and from both urban and rural areas. Helene Robbe, a French girl who lives in London and has a penchant for roller-skating, expresses her club interest in the April 29, 1922, edition, though she worries only Americans are allowed to join. "I would like very much to become a member, but of course I don't suppose you want any foreigners," she laments ("The Defender Junior," April 29, 1922, 14). But, undeterred, she writes, "I am filling in the application, and if I am not eligible to become a member you can just tear it up" (14). Besides geography, correspondence also evidences the variance in social circumstances, with notes written by children living in agricultural regions and those attending private schools. Allen James from Texas describes his farm life, telling readers, "I can pick cotton and cut stalks" ("Chicago Defender Junior," April 23, 1921, 5). He also indicates that animals are an essential part of country childhood, a feature that might excite the imagination of city children: "I have a pig and a calf and bulldog and my dog kills all of the rats she can catch" (5). Sixth-grader Susie Perry details her unique experiences living in the Tuskegee Institute community in Alabama, which would probably sound thrilling to children unfamiliar with college campuses. She and her younger sister "run to get the Defender when we see Captain Drye coming with it. He is the band master of the Tuskegee Inst. Band" ("Chicago Defender Junior," July 2, 1921, 6). The range of childhood material and social contexts shown in the Defender Junior provided a means for black youth to reconceive the often one-dimensional depictions of African Americans in literature, history, and mass culture.

The geographical diversity of the readers indicates that expectations for girlhood and boyhood vary regionally, particularly between black children living in urban and rural parts of the county. A letter from Jewel in Louisiana illustrates how she flouts gender convention. She recalls a trip to Shreveport when "my uncle took me into the woods and we killed birds and snakes" and "the next day we went fishing and ... I caught the first fish" ("Chicago Defender Junior," June 11, 1921, 8). For Jewel and her family with whom she participates in hunting and fishing, the woods are a place for both boys and girls to explore and even enact violence through "kill[ing] birds and snakes." Jewel shows her proficiency in activities deemed traditionally masculine by catching "the first fish."

Perhaps because of the lack of outlets for African American young persons in the early twentieth century, the Bud Billiken readers and contributors ranged from children not yet in grade school to those in their late teens. With few resources targeted to a young black audience, a publication that was also composed by its primary demographic would have undeniable appeal across the age spectrum. Thus, club members included very young readers such as Edna Mae Patrick, a "country girl" from Aurora, Nebraska, turning "seven years old next month" who "go[es] to school every day," and Allie Simmons from Galveston, "a little girl five years old" who is "not old enough to go to public school" ("Chicago Defender Junior," April 23, 1921, 5; "Chicago Defender Junior," June 4, 1921, 8). But the Defender Junior also attracted teenagers such as Helene Robbe, the seventeen-year-old French girl living in London, and Katie C. Murphy, a student attending Morris Brown College in Atlanta, who is "down to hard work" and "kept quite busy" at school ("The Defender Junior," Nov. 15, 1924, A3). However, Katie is "never distracted from my duties as a member of the Bud Billiken club" (A3). For her, the fellowship provided by the Defender Junior figures as an essential part of life, regardless her demanding college schedule.

In a time before social media, online forums, and even ubiquitous telephone service, the artifice of the Defender Junior offered a platform for social interaction and social creative endeavor. Through its visible apparatus, readers could absorb the idea that they had a voice and a community, both of which they had the power to fashion. The machinery of the Defender Junior itself helped forge identity through encouraging creativity, yet it also gave readers a means to reach out to one another. The newspaper enabled black youth to find friends to combat the cultural and psychological effects of geographic isolation. Responding to this distinct social need among African American children, as well as the desire among youth for pen pals, the Defender Junior solicited addresses to publish so that readers could write to one another. "This space is given to the members of the Billiken Club so that they may become acquainted," a section headlined "Addresses Wanted" states in the Jan. 14, 1922, edition ("The Defender Junior," Jan. 14, 1922, 18). The section goes on to facilitate communication between readers, with "[ad]dresses given below," asking that the "names indicated please take notice and answer" (18). For some Billiken Club members, the weekly page and the letters received from other members became a lifeline during periods of desolation. Wilhemina Stewart of Montgomery, "a student at State Normal school," writes a letter to Bud and the Defender Junior to help raise her spirits ("The Defender Junior," Nov. 15, 1924, B3). "I am very lonesome today. I thought I would drop a line to you," Wilhemina writes, ending her letter with, "Please tell all the Billikens that I am in very great need of mail" (B3). The sense of inclusion and understanding amid a wide, unseen network outside the confines of their everyday lived experience serves as a means of renewal, not only emotional, but creative. Wilhemina discerns that writing—specifically, writing to her club—will ameliorate her state of mind. Washington D.C. Billiken Juanita Johnson articulated this idea through a poem she sent to the Defender Junior in 1921:

> When you are lonely and don't know what to do,
> When you must admit that you are feeling blue,
> Take your pen in hand, my dear child, I entreat,
> And write the B. B. Club something nice and sweet.
> Your blues will depart, I'll surely guarantee.
> You'll cheer up at once, for so it is with me.
> ("Chicago Defender Junior," July 2, 1921, 6)

The page and the club build community through open interaction with artifice—the intertwined, overt manipulation of art and social constructs—as facilitated by the newspaper. This embrace of artifice reveals the capacity for individuals or groups to create social change, as pursued by outlets such as the *Chicago Defender*. Moreover, the consciousness of belonging to the Billiken Club, of being part of something nationally recognized in print, empowers black youth to "take ... pen in hand" and give expression to their thoughts and feelings. The black newspaper becomes a symbolic vehicle for African American children to "make" news and enact social change by deconstructing and refashioning the artifice that surrounds them.

Poetry and the Defender Junior

Perhaps because of its obvious constructedness, with its acknowledged literary forms and formulas, poetry became a reliable means of interacting with artifice for Bud Billiken Club members. Indeed, many of the contributors thought a poetic submission was expected, with members vowing, "Next week I am going to send you a poem" or "I will send you a nice poem next time" ("Chicago Defender Junior," June 11, 1921, 8; June 25, 1921, 8). But Susie Perry, the Defender Junior reader living on the Tuskegee campus, asserts, "I will not send a poem until I fully understand your club" ("Chicago Defender Junior," July 2, 1921, 6). Dorothy Edwards of New Orleans, meanwhile, sees the Billiken Club as an opportunity to improve her verse: "I am not a good poetry writer but there is nothing like trying, because if at first you don't succeed, try again" ("The Defender Junior," Jan. 14, 1922, 18). The emphasis on poetry as a means of personal and literary expression in the Defender Junior reflects social and cultural movements in the African American artistic communities and the education system during the early twentieth century, and it demonstrates how black children readily began to both emulate traditional models and revise them to more accurately represent their particular reality or creative vision.

In regard to developments in the literary scene and school curricula for the black community during this period, scholars note the influential role of African American poet Paul Laurence Dunbar (1872–1906) in mainstream and children's culture through both his work and life story. Kate Capshaw Smith elaborates on this point, explaining that "[a]ttention to Dunbar allows us to understand how children's writers in the 1920s and 1930s made use of his biography and his verse in order to spearhead their own versions of black identity, southern history, and artistic experimentation" (113). Dunbar's poetry provided a "white-approved version of folk culture" while also giving black Americans a literary voice that resonated with their lived experiences (Smith 121). However, Dunbar and his persona vexed writers of the Harlem Renaissance, since "his mode of dialect writing was absolutely repellent to many New Negro writers," Smith tells us, adding that "rejection of Dunbar became a sign of aesthetic modernity" (112). Nevertheless, "Dunbar's life story offered child readers an example of the kind of social advancement and success endorsed by the elite thinkers of the New Negro movement" (Smith 117–18). This is all to say that while the Defender Junior (as well as, certainly, *The Brownies' Book*) showcased some of the racial-uplift ideology circulating in African American schools, literature, and institutions, it also served as a space in which youth could experiment with these traditional forms to discover their individual voices.

In many poems published during the early years of *Chicago Defender*'s youth section, the content and form echo those of the poems that children would probably have encountered in school. The influence of Dunbar's traditional work permeates each issue. The poem "Springtime" submitted by Elmone K. Seals of West Virginia, for example, replicates the romanticized conflation of childhood and nature seen in a Dunbar poem such as "Winter Song" (1905). The narrator in Dunbar's poem uses singsong rhythm and rhyme to brighten the potentially dark moods of winter, detailing the playfulness and wonder of the natural landscape. Calling attention to the "little white birds thro' the winter-kissed air" and the squirrel as he "munches his store in the old hollow tree," Dunbar's narrator endorses the delight to be found in the snowy scene, intensified by the final chorus lines:

> Then heigho for the flying snow!
> Over the whitened roads we go,
> With pulses that tingle,
> And sleigh-bells a-jingle
> For winter's white birds here's a cheery heigho! (4–5)

Similarly, Elmone K. Seals's "Springtime" sees the natural cycle of the seasons and its accompanying ecology as a means for buoying spirits:

> The brooks go murmuring by,
> With blue reflections from the sky,
> And birds go singing, singing,
> Cheerful hearts they're bringing. ("Chicago Defender Junior," June 4, 1921, 8)

The narrator locates a simple, understated power in observing the aesthetic and aural beauty in the routine events of a spring day. Both "Winter Song" and "Springtime" suggest that those who can appreciate nature will receive rewards of "cheery heigho[s]" and "cheerful hearts." This theme, while a traditional poetic trope, would understandably make an impression on African Americans in the early twentieth century; though the political and social systems may be unjust, grace exists in abundance in the natural world.

Some may unfairly dismiss poems such as "Springtime" (and "Winter Song," for that matter) as merely mimetic of the traditional verse of white poets, despite its subtle advocacy for alternative forms of agency. But the poetry published in the Defender Junior gave children a written form and an outlet to express the confusion and disappointment resulting from any number of social circumstances confronting black youth. Moreover, it emphasized the reader's potential to be an artificer, whether of poetry or social change. In January 1922, the section printed a poem written by Lillian W. Osten from Union City, Tennessee, that wrestles with the difficulty children undergo as a result of conforming to gender conventions. Lillian, the speaker of the poem, proclaims: "If I were a man, / Oh, the things I'd do. / I'd be a sailor / And wear a uniform of blue" ("The Defender Junior," Jan. 21, 1922, 18). Believing such vocations wholly impossible because of her gender, the narrator momentarily finds solace through imagining the things she could experience if she were "a man" in the jobs of "sailor," "farmer," or "mason." But the poem also obliquely hints at the racial obstacles to gainful, gratifying employment. The last stanza presents the idea of the girl being a "soldier" and "fight[ing] for Uncle Sam," but then quickly returns to reality: "But such is life, / I must be what I am" (18). The abrupt move from the phrase "fight for Uncle Sam" to that of "But such is life" and the poem's concluding sentiment of resignation evokes the nation's state of racial discord. While a woman or girl "fight[ing] for Uncle Sam" may have seemed particularly impossible to Lillian in 1922, African American men could serve in certain areas of the military under enforced policies of discrimination and segregation. The narrator realizes the paradoxical situation of "fight[ing] for Uncle Sam," who maintains racial and gender disparity, and she humbly, forlornly acquiesces to "be what I am." The ambiguous blank spaces of poetry provide another lyrical language, one that works in concert with the written words of the Defender poets, together capturing the complex realities of black childhood.

Community, Commerce, and Childhood Creativity in the Defender Junior

While the Defender Junior's advocacy of artifice underscored the overriding social-change agenda of the *Chicago Defender*, it also had indisputable commercial appeal for the newspaper. Through the section, the *Defender* not only established a loyal base of potential lifelong readers, it turned club members into *Defender* evangelists, many of whom actually helped sell the paper in their communities. The relationship of artifice, commodity, and community, in terms of the Billiken readership, becomes blurred, since a sense of African American youth identity accordingly corresponds to growth in *Defender* sales— the more a product sells, the more discernible its audience becomes. In both prose and poetry, Bud Billiken members again and again reiterate the importance of the club and the *Defender* to their everyday lives and their race as a whole, thus working to mutually shape both their community and the newspaper commodity.

Readers often sent their wishes to join the Bud Billiken Club while also emphasizing their allegiance to the *Defender*. "As I was reading the Chicago Defender a lovely paper of our Race [sic], I came across some beautiful poems by some of the members of your club," writes Ruth McBride, a nine-year-old from Alabama ("Chicago Defender Junior," June 18, 1921, 8). She makes sure to mention that her "mother gets the Defender every week" (8). It seems that for Ruth and other Defender Junior readers, part of membership instinctually includes reaffirming the work done by the "lovely paper of our Race" and stressing a type of brand loyalty, as Ruth does through citing her mother's habit of newspaper purchase.

Most interesting about these displays of praise and fidelity is that the child contributors show an understanding of the newspaper's artifice and how it can be empowering. Because the *Chicago Defender* extols the use of artifice, its child readers intuit how to become skillful artificers themselves. Through the processes of crafting their letters and poetry, club members certify the truth of the *Chicago Defender* for other young readers. Ten-year-old Allen Leon Wright, who had recently moved from Mississippi to live in Chicago with his aunt, deems Chicago "the greatest place in the world for children," and like his aunt, plans on being a lifetime *Defender* reader ("Chicago Defender Junior," June 11, 1921, 8). Allen goes on to articulate the newspaper's prominent role in the black community through a poem, which begins with the following stanzas:

> The people are roaming over Chicago,
> The masculine and feminine gender.
> But the only way to get the news
> Is by reading the Chicago Defender.
> I read the papers every day,
> Describing the legal tender,
> But if you wish to know about the South
> Just read the Chicago Defender. (8)

On its face, these lines read like an advertisement in child's verse. While they certainly convey a rhetorical function similar to that of ad copy, these stanzas also point toward the social and historical conditions of the 1920s. Allen, or the "I" narrator, "read[s] the papers every day" that contain "legal tender," implying that he reads the mainstream titles published from and for the perspective of white America. The line "describing the legal tender" is immediately followed by the oppositional conjunction "But" to suggest that national "legal tender" omits the pervasive injustice, both obvious and insidious, occurring to African Americans across the country, and particularly in the South. The *Defender*, then, may operate according to dictates of capitalistic enterprise, but it also serves distinct social and political needs that ten-year-old Allen detects. He knows "the story about John S. Williams"—a Georgia plantation owner who maintained a peonage system of labor and who was convicted of murdering eleven of his black workers in 1921 (Stowe 194–97)—"Is found in the Chicago Defender" because, as his verse communicates, the newspaper prints the news of black America not reported in the period's predominant outlets (8).

In the Nov. 15, 1924, issue, reader Katherine Mercer asserts her devotion to the newspaper even more emphatically through an acrostic poem using the words "Chicago Defender."[10] The use of "Omnipotent," "Eternal," "Righteousness," "Infinite," and "Charity" seemingly elevates the newspaper to a place worthy of religious worship. For Katherine, the *Defender* carries Biblical importance through its dissemination of "truth which tears the veil of ignorance and unsophistication from the eyes" (A3). The sentiments of Allen and Katherine signify how the Bud Billiken Club became an invaluable promotional tool for the *Chicago Defender* and its sales. Yet their words likewise show us that disentangling the purposes of social reform and financial profit is impossible. Moreover, the club shows the multifarious nature of the newspaper and its intricately entwined relationship with child readers, each relying on the other to create and propagate social change through embracing artifice.

The Task Ahead

Bud Billiken's legacy, which continues in Chicago through the welcomed, unabashed artifice of the annual Bud Billiken Parade, documents the story of African American youth creating their own community and fostering an audience for children's literature through artfully shaping the newspaper into children's literature itself. The newspaper's youth section served as a space where young people could experiment with the powers of artifice along social, cultural, and creative lines. And while momentous work has been done in civil rights, social reform, and cultural awareness of racial disparity, large numbers of minority youth continue to become victims or perpetrators of violence, often as a result of getting lost in the nexus of institutional, political, and legal policies that more readily accommodate economically and socially advantaged families. In 2014 the Bud Billiken Parade witnessed its first incident of gun violence, reflecting the tumultuous socioeconomic conditions and circumstances that continue to plague African American youth on Chicago's South Side, as well as other minority youth throughout the United States. The *Chicago Tribune* reported that "the shooting of two teenagers just off the parade's main route sent some families running for cover—and left others angry that this longtime African-American tradition had been violated" (Black n. p.).

A 2014 study from the U.S. Department of Education Office for Civil Rights found that nationwide there still exists a "pattern of inequality on a number of fronts, with race as the dividing factor" in public schools in regard to matters of course offerings, teacher performance, and student expulsion, among others (Rich n. p.). For black youths, the expression of curiosity and creativity exemplified in the Defender Junior has become a privilege rather than a basic right of childhood. In exploring the gulf between the childhood examples found in the Defender Junior and those of many at-risk communities today, we may find solutions to bridge them, and thus potentially return to a semblance of the vision and message presented at the dawn of the Harlem Renaissance. In recovering the cultural work of the Defender Junior, we find a record of youth culture in the making, one that exposes the intricate links among identity, community, and writing, and also exposes the ultimate truths *of the processes* of social and creative construction. The early twentieth century witnessed African American children forging their own literature and community through the newspaper to authenticate their individual and cultural selves. The technological advances of today's media and literary landscape allow for infinite spaces in which young people can discover, deconstruct, rearrange, or redefine their identities and communities through textual, visual, and audio discourses—if only they are given access and example. Of course, academia and media cannot offer any easy answers or instant solutions to the issues of diverse racial representations in youth media; the gradual evolution of the original Defender Junior into a page more focused on school news and events perhaps reflects that. Throughout issues of the *Defender* in 1975, the newspaper ran an advertisement soliciting renewed interest in the Bud Billiken Club, which, the writer reminds younger, unfamiliar readers, "had pen pals ... and wrote stories," among other things ("Other 3—No Title"). However, the *Defender* has maintained youth participation through the annual parade. But in terms of youth media and representation, we must continue, determinedly and doggedly, to invest in and advocate for the necessary long-term efforts to cultivate such development at the individual, local, and systemic levels.

Only months before his death in July 2014, Walter Dean Myers wrote a column for *the New York Times* entitled "Where Are the People of Color in Children's Books?" Myers relates a statistic from the Cooperative Children's Book Center at the University of Wisconsin: "[o]f 3,200 children's books published in 2013, just 93 were about black people" (n.p.). Myers goes on to detail the difficulty that he experienced during his youth after realizing that the novels he read in no way reflected his social reality. "As I discovered who I was, a black teenager in a white-dominated world, I saw that these characters, these lives, were not mine," writes Myers (n.p.). He recalls that he then "wanted" and "needed" "to become an integral and valued part of the mosaic that I saw around me" (n.p.). Despite his own efforts and those of other writers, Myers still must ask, "Where are black children going to get a sense of who they are and what they can be?" (n.p.). He ends by simply observing, "There is work to be done" (n.p.). To Myers and his readership, a young Bud Billikens might have responded, "Now, Billikens, all, you see the task we have ahead of us—get busy" ("Chicago Defender Junior," Jan. 7, 1922, 8). During the early twentieth century, the *Chicago Defender* extended its open agenda as a newspaper attempting to advance racial equality by inviting young readers into the process of artifice. The Chicago Defender Junior helped create a legion of artificers, youth able to decode and refashion the creative and cultural apparatus that organizes and distributes power. It is through this exposure and embrace of artifice that American children's literature continues its role as social change agent in the twenty-first century.

Conclusion

"I Want to Know Everything"

Harriet the Spy and New Journalism

In 1963, *Esquire* magazine published "There Goes (Varoom! Varoom!) That Kandy-Kolored (Thphhhhhh!) Tangerine-Flake Streamline Baby (Rahghhh!) Around the Bend (Brummmmmmmmmmmmmmm)," an article by Tom Wolfe that peers into the burgeoning American interest in custom cars, in particular the teen interest in custom cars. That piece, defined by Wolfe's self-narration and intellectually whimsical style, ushered in the New Journalism movement that he and writers such as Gay Talese, Terry Southern, Truman Capote, Hunter S. Thompson, George Plimpton, and Joan Didion would help define in the years that followed. "The first good look I had at customized cars was at an event called a 'Teen Fair,' held in Burbank, a suburb of Los Angeles beyond Hollywood," begins Wolfe's feature, which was both celebrated and reviled by his contemporaries. He immediately establishes himself in the story and outlines the peculiar positions that reporters find themselves in when they are on assignment, including the ways in which journalists can be easily swayed and undermined by their sources. "Tex Smith, from *Hot Rod Magazine*, who brought me over to the place, is trying to lead me to the customized-car exhibit—'Tom. I want you to see this car that Bill Cushenberry built, The Silhouette,'" writes Wolfe of his initial tour guide, who conveniently tries to provide Wolfe with choice interviewees ("Kandy-Kolored" 77). Instead of focusing on the exhibit, however, Wolfe attempts to derive wider meaning from what he deems a fascinatingly bizarre social phenomenon amid "the noise and peripheral motion and the inchoate leching you are liable to be doing, what with the bouffant nymphets rocketing all over the place" ("Kandy-Kolored" 78).

Wolfe refuses to present a straightforward depiction of the Teen Fair and instead carries readers through a cultural investigation into the philosophical significance of the American custom car. Instead of composing a detailed description of the event that abides by the reporter's creed of objectivity, Wolfe makes his journalistic process part of the article. In so doing, he exposes the

89

artifice of presumed objectivity. In an essay that ultimately functions as a meditation of the existential import of form as expressed through the customization of cars "[I]f you watched anything at this fair very long, you kept noticing the same thing. These kids are absolutely maniacal about form. They are practically religious about it." ("Kandy-Kolored" 78)—Wolfe destabilizes the traditional journalistic form in his documentation of the knowledge process itself.

During the early years of New Journalism's experiments with form and storytelling, fictional New Yorker Harriet M. Welsch entered the consciousness of children's literature and popular culture, unsettling the conventional heroine model. The precocious—and, at times, acidic—eleven-year-old in Louise Fitzhugh's *Harriet the Spy* (1964) maintains the lofty mission to know "[e]verything in the world, everything, everything" (24). Harriet attempts this feat through her spying and subsequent reporting of said spying into her notorious notebook. For instance, after Harriet listens in on the telephone conversation of privileged housewife Mrs. Agatha Plumber, who declares that the "*secret* of *life*" is to "*take* to your *bed*" and "refuse to leave it for *anything* or *anybody*," Harriet takes to her notebook to both chronicle and make sense of her findings (45; emphasis original). She eventually determines for herself the necessity of individual work and accomplishment, convinced of Mrs. Plumber's foolishness because of her seeming lack of ambition. For Harriet, Mrs. Plumber's inability to act or "decid[e] on a profession" renders her a woman without passion—and therefore "dum[b]" (45). After spying on Mrs. Plumber, Harriet uses her notebook to work through the implications of Mrs. Plumber's situation: "HOW CAN YOU WORK LYING DOWN? ... I GUESS SHE JUST LIVES OFF HER HUSBAND'S MONEY. DOES MY MOTHER MOOCH OFF MY FATHER? I'LL NEVER DO THAT" (46). People who occupy too much of their time with unadulterated idleness like Mrs. Plumber are "dull" to Harriet because "when people don't do anything, they don't think anything, and when they don't think anything there's nothing to think about them" (57, 45). In documenting Harriet's spying and providing selections of Harriet's recorded observations, the novel shows her development of self and societal understanding through her reporting and her writing. But *Harriet the Spy* does more than simply tout the value of writing.

Throughout the preceding chapters, *Cub Reporters* has asserted that our literary texts both reflect and shape our ideas about American childhood, and that the intersections between journalism, children's literature, and artifice in particular have affected these ideas. To conclude, I want to show how this dialogue of artifice continued past the Golden Age. When contextualized within the New Journalism movement of the 1960s, *Harriet the Spy* evidences the sustained relationship between American children's literature and journalism, a relationship rooted in the use of artifice and the late-nineteenth-century response to the cultural role of the newspaper. Curious and creative Harriet functions as a reporter of artifice for readers as she uncovers and interacts with the artifice, both social and creative, that surrounds her. The text thus shows readers that if social conventions, cultural ideologies, and imaginative endeavors are artifice (or products of artifice), they can be reconstructed; the text promotes the investigation, deconstruction, and reinvention of individual and social realities. In the New Journalism work of Tom Wolfe and others—long-form journalism that is today familiar and taught in journalism and creative-writing programs across the country—we find an unmasking of journalism's conventions, similar to the unmasking of artifice that children's literature undertook beginning in the Golden Age. With *Harriet the Spy* and Tom Wolfe, we find a validation of artifice and a rejection of existential, intellectual, or creative passivity.

Harriet's "profession" of spying is a profession of curiosity—her attempt to "know everything" (281, 24). "LIFE IS A GREAT MYSTERY," Harriet surmises, and her mission is to solve it (97). Harriet, as a critical observer and agent of curiosity, shares a liminal space with the figure of the journalistic reporter, particularly the avant-garde representatives of New Journalism such as Wolfe and Thompson. They are outsider figures. But because of the ghettoized status of children's literature and journalism as ugly step-relatives to literary fiction, their position enabled them to experiment with convention, form, and expectations during the fledgling days of the civil rights movement and second-wave feminism.[1] Taken together, New Journalism and *Harriet the Spy* become explorations of artifice, of how story and knowledge are created. Ultimately, they suggest that only through open exploration of and collaboration with artifice can we "know everything," or anything at all.

During New Journalism's development, the profession grappled with its formal polemic and its ability to accurately render truth through mimetic reconstruction and careful reporting. This response mines territory that American children's literature had been reacting to nearly a century before. Here, I consider how *Harriet the Spy* and early examples of New Journalism show us how American children's literature and journalism have both absorbed and shaped each other over the course of the century. The intersections between children's literature and journalism in the 1960s evince a cultural disavowal of singular fact and an affirmation of artifice and the individual creative experience, and consequently, allow for confrontation of ideological beliefs regarding childhood, truth, and the human condition. Having discerned the ongoing discussion between children's literature and journalism, we can begin to ask more productive questions about our constructs of modern childhood and adulthood. And questions, as we glean from reading *Harriet the Spy* in the context of New Journalism, can be more essential than answers.

Harriet the Spy in the Popular and Critical Imagination

Before analyzing the relationship between New Journalism and *Harriet the Spy*, a brief overview of the novel's cultural import and influence, particularly in the world of children's literature, helps illuminate the significance of this particular reciprocity. *Harriet the Spy* offers a productive study in regard to ideologies of childhood because of the novel's polarizing effect on readers. Fitzhugh's work has secured canonical status in children's literature and popular culture, yet it also has drawn its share of detractors over the past fifty-plus years. However, opposition to the novel largely stemmed from librarians, not children (Bernstein 832). "[Y]oung readers loved Harriet," Neva Grant reports in a 2008 feature for National Public Radio (Grant). She writes that in "the 1960s and 70s, young girls formed *Harriet the Spy* clubs. They dressed up like her and spied on their parents" (Grant).[2] Yet some people find Harriet problematic or unlikable because, simply put, she writes mean things in her notebook. Many of Harriet's entries are unpleasant, such as when she writes that she would "smash" a "very noisy child who tried to read [her] notebooks" (97), or when she says that Marion Hawthorne will "grow up into a lady Hitler ... if she doesn't watch it" (184). She also insists that one of the things "to do about" Pinky Whitehead is to "tear his pants off and laugh at him" (184). When Harriet's private writing is made public, her classmates ostracize her for these remarks, even though they may be true. Arguably, children (and adult) readers embrace both Harriet and the novel for this very reason: Harriet writes and says the things they actually think and feel. Moreover, *Harriet the Spy* conveys the overwhelming lack of agency available to children in twentieth-century America, yet provides redemption by means of Harriet's disruption of the status quo via her spying and writing. In other words, Harriet shows young readers how to unearth, assemble, and craft new meaning into their lives.

Despite initial critical praise, *Harriet the Spy* received backlash from librarians shortly after its publication because it invited investigation into the parameters of childhood and presented the possibilities of children being complex, intellectual, and sometimes moody. Robin Bernstein relates that although "[i]nitially, most critics hailed *Harriet*'s humour and originality" the novel "became the object of widespread criticism" after a 1965 *Horn Book* review by Ruth Hill Viguers (832). Viguers questions the depiction of Harriet and the use of the term "realism" to describe the book, forcing her to wonder, "'Are there really no amiable children?'" (qtd. in Bernstein 832).[3] Viguers's association of *Harriet the Spy* with realism anticipates the "new realism" period of children's literature and the beginning of the young adult literature category, often marked by the publication of S. E. Hinton's *The Outsiders* (1967). Cathryn M. Mercier points out the difficulty scholars and publishers have had historically in defining realist literature for young people, "given realism's function in separating children's literature from literature for adults" (198). In the late 1960s and early 1970s, the publishing category of "young adult" cemented itself through first-person narratives such as *The Outsiders* and Judy Blume's *Are You There God? It's Me, Margaret.* (1970), in which the acknowledged construct of the protagonists' narratives establishes each novel's existence. Margaret is writing in her diary, Ponyboy is composing an essay for his English class. For readers, this recognition of how writing grants individual agency encourages investigation and reconstruction of the creative and social artifice in their own lives.

As a precursor to young adult literature's new realism, *Harriet the Spy* has been a point of continual interest among children's literature scholars, especially given its protagonist's ability to forcibly refashion her role in the world. J. D. Stahl argues that Fitzhugh's novel illustrates children's subversive powers of social reconstruction through Harriet, "who appropriates adult forms of literacy and transforms them to suit her own purposes" (120). According to Stahl, the novel depicts "the subsumption of the adult's reality by the child" (121). Lissa Paul reads Harriet as an archetypal feminist writer who "prefers a small-scale form of writing (the private notebook)" and "juggles her role in society (her popularity with her classmates) with her role as a writer (which demands selfishness)" (67). And while "she is concerned with being truthful," Harriet "ultimately discovers that that necessitates lying," and thus she decides "that domestic gossip constitutes a valid form of fiction" (67).

My contention transects the arguments put forth by Stahl and Paul in that I see *Harriet the Spy* as corroding the barrier between "being truthful" and "lying," between the fantastical realms of the Alice books and the actual spaces of contemporary New York, to show and repurpose artifice. Artifice *is* the only means of "being truthful," according to the novel. More specifically, through the explicit grappling with truth and the writing process, and the overt acknowledgment of writing constructs, *Harriet* extends the established conversation between children's literature and journalism. As Paul indicates, Harriet comes to realize that there exists truth in fiction and deceit in facts, and that she must discern what is true for her. As a spy, writer, and reporter, she uncovers the ways in which power structures—school, her parents, the newspaper—sometimes hide artifice to secure authority.

The New Journalism

By the 1970s, New Journalism had established itself within mainstream media outlets.[4] In 1973, Tom Wolfe, along with E. W. Johnson, edited the essay collection *The New Journalism*, which includes seminal pieces published over the course of the previous decade from the genre's definitive writers, such as Talese, Thompson, and Wolfe. The book's introduction serves as hybrid history of and manifesto for the movement, with Wolfe explaining its organic evolution in his opening lines. He writes, "I doubt if many of the aces I will be extolling in this story went into journalism with the faintest notion of creating a 'new' journalism, a 'higher' journalism, or even a mildly improved variety" (3). In other words, New Journalism developed through an unconscious cultural osmosis rather than an organized, concerted response to the inadequacies of contemporary journalism. Nevertheless, Wolfe describes the impasse at which journalists found themselves, given the generic principle of journalism itself as both factual and artistic. Newsrooms, according to Wolfe, were composed of reporters either competing for scoops or vying for the title of "Best Feature Writer in Town" ("New Journalism" 5). Herein seemed to lie part of the problem—writers saw the newsroom as a place of limbo since the "final triumph was known as The Novel" (5). However, "[t]hat was Someday, you understand ... Meanwhile, these dreamboaters were in there banging away in every place in American that had a newspaper" (5). Journalism maintaining a second-class image of itself surely limited its scope and effectiveness, as well as its craft, if not its veracity.

The New Journalism of the 1960s attempts to reinvigorate and legitimate the profession's claims on "truth" by abandoning the pretense of objectivity. *It embraces artifice* in a manner akin to that of Golden Age children's literature. In fashioning journalistic writing that details the investigative journey itself, and by incorporating unconventional, myriad discourses, the New Journalist conveys the inconsequence of prescribed, formulaic answers. Kevin Kerrane, in a prefatory piece to the anthology *The Art of Fact: A Historical Anthology of Literary Fiction* (1998), remarks on Wolfe's focus on "stylistic innovations" of journalistic form such as "scene-by-scene narration, dramatic dialogue, experiments in point of view, and attention to the symbolic details of social life," but indicates that the turbulent landscape of 1960s America necessitated the radical form employed by Wolfe and New Journalism (17). "[M]uch of this fresh writing was, first and foremost, a direct response to the transforming events of the era:

war protests, race riots, assassinations, and countercultural challenges to all proprieties," Kerrane asserts, because the "'genteel voice' of traditional reportage was no longer sufficient to articulate public reality" (18). Meanwhile, critics have maintained that Wolfe's New Journalism "is a facile, shallow, even immoral form which is neither realistic nor valid literature" (Hellmann 416). John Hellmann gets to the heart of the matter, contending that "New [J]ournalism and fabulation are in fact not only creative responses to the same problematic state of realism, but are also significantly related approaches to its possible solution," that being the overt acknowledgement of the "illusion of reality" (416).

Troubling our expectations of form, Wolfe's New Journalist documents how revealing and rendering artifice leads us to ascertain the meaning of cultural ideologies and governing social systems. Authenticity can only be achieved by recognizing the process itself, not simply its product. "I had the feeling, rightly or wrongly, that I was doing things no one had ever done before in journalism," Wolfe says, noting that he wanted to access "Pushkin's sense [of] 'looking at all things afresh,' as if for the first time, without the constant intimidation of being aware of what others had already done" ("New Journalism" 20).[5] Wolfe suggests that the analysis and interpretation of culture, society, power structures, and daily existence have a particular potency when conducted "as if for the first time," in the same manner as that of a curious young girl surveying and scrutinizing her New York neighborhood.

Rather than ignoring the innumerable, fractured methods by which we piece together meaning in an increasingly complicated world, New Journalism takes advantage of them to disrupt hegemonic narratives of national and social identity. Wolfe walks readers through his own interrogation process in a way that exposes the machinations of construction. "Kandy-Kolored Tangerine-Flake Streamline Baby" guides the reader along, annotating the accumulation of critical observations as retold by Wolfe in conversational language. In so doing, Wolfe unassumingly shows the capitalistic interests of the car industry at work:

> Anyway, we are back at the Teen Fair.... As they tell me about the Ford Custom Car Caravan, I can see that Ford has begun to comprehend this teen-age style of life and its potential. The way Ford appears to figure it is this: Thousands of kids are getting hold of cars.... If Ford can get them hooked on Fords now, after the kids are married they'll buy new Fords. Even the kids who aren't fulltime car nuts themselves will be influenced by which car is considered "boss." They use that word a lot, "boss." (80)

A feature on a seemingly innocuous "Teen Fair" functions as a lens through which the power dynamics between youth and corporations, as well as the influence that each wields, are casually drawn out. The article becomes *about* the composition of an experience as it happens, intertwining the construction of thought and writing, the same dissection of truth we see in *Harriet the Spy*.

In *The Electric Kool-Aid Acid Test* (1968), Wolfe continues to experiment with form and the construction of thought and writing by knitting together various modes of discourse to replicate the chaos of not only a drug-induced hallucination, but the larger social disorder of the United States. The text, which documents time Wolfe spent with Ken Kesey and the Merry Pranksters, shifts between perspectives without clear delineation, leaving the reader to make sense of the confusion. For example, in addition to incorporating linguistic playfulness, scenes begin without indication of who is speaking and without clear understanding of whose voice is the supposed "objective" journalistic voice:

> Haul ass, Kesey. Move. *Scram. Split flee hide vanish disintegrate*. Like *run*. Rrrrrrrrrrrrrrrrrrrrrev revrevrevrevrevrevrevrevrev or are we gonna have just a late Mexican re-run of the scene on the rooftop in San Francisco and sit here with the motor spinning and watch with fascination while the cops they climb up once again to *come git you*—(204)

Immediately following this passage, the text presents another voice without explanation:

> THEY JUST OPENED THE DOOR DOWN BELOW, ROTOR ROOTER, SO YOU HAVE MAYBE 45 SECONDS ASSUMING THEY BE SLOW AND SNEAKY AND SURE ABOUT IT ("From *The Electric Kool-Aid Acid Test*" 204)

Wolfe disorients readers with his Faulknerian employment of stream of consciousness in a genre that purports to be real, factual—true. Instead, using his interviews, observations of the escapades of the Merry Pranksters, and Kesey's own writing, Wolfe creates narrative chaos to replicate the existential chaos of Kesey's psychological being and legal situation as the threat of a mandatory prison sentence looms over him.[6] In essence, the text abandons the pretense of coherent linearity, forcing readers to create meaning for themselves. The text also functions to serve as a reminder that journalism—charged with identifying and crafting coherent linearity—has always been based in creativity. For Wolfe and others of the New Journalism school, their profession seemingly becomes an advocacy for the facts of artifice.

Spying and Writing Truth in *Harriet the Spy*

In its shared ethos with New Journalism, *Harriet the Spy* encourages youth agency by showing the necessity for individual investigation to determine knowledge and meaning. By accentuating the constructedness of Harriet's own being, the text invites readers to write their own truths and embrace their own unique experiences of childhood. For Harriet, part of that creative process is the engineering of her routines. The emphasis on routine highlights both its arbitrariness and its utility, and it reinforces how Harriet's routines help her make meaning of the world. Harriet relishes her routines. She delights in eating a tomato sandwich every day for lunch. She loves indulging in her daily afternoon snack of cake and milk at precisely 3:40 p.m. And she lives for maintaining her "regular spy route," which she attends to each day after school, armed with her composition notebook (33). When she attends to her spy route, Harriet observes and takes notes about people living close to her neighborhood. In this, she understands herself to be doing her *job*. After the household cook offhandedly tells her to "go out and play," an irate Harriet corrects her: "I do not go out to PLAY, I go out to WORK!" (39). Harriet undermines the categorical definitions of work and play, showing readers how such categories can be reinterpreted. She suggests that there is nothing innate or static in regard to such organizational artifice, but instead that meaning can be gleaned from considering the application and relevance of these categories.

Rather than distinct conceptions of "play" and "work," it is curiosity and its expression that animate all of Harriet's actions, defining her understanding of people and society. She does not discern individuals by their age or station so much as she judges them by their drive and enthusiasm for knowledge. She has internalized advice from her nanny, Ole Golly, who shows a desire for knowledge in her reading and quoting of classic literature, even if Ole Golly herself does not always understand her recitations from Dostoyevsky and Henry James. Harriet's formulation of work derives from Ole Golly's sentiment that "PEOPLE WHO LOVE THEIR WORK LOVE LIFE" (71). Thus, for Harriet, there is no real distinction between her own work and play—though in others, such as lazy housewife Agatha Plumber, she deems play to be a state of idleness and passivity.

The existential satisfaction Harriet derives from her work and play manifests through her writing. Her notebook containing her field reporting notes serves as a space to work through her observations, insights, and emotional responses, and proves as essential to her as her tomato-sandwich sustenance.

After being nearly caught by Mrs. Plumber, for instance, Harriet "careened around the corner. Panting, she sat on some steps and took out her book" (46). The discoveries Harriet makes from her spying can only be validated and have wider application after she crafts them into the larger significance contained in her composition notebook. Indeed, the central crisis of the novel results from the notebook prohibition forced on her by Mr. and Mrs. Welsch. After Harriet's parents regulate her notebook writing, she experiences intense anxiety until she can at last record and synthesize her findings:

> She grabbed up the pen and felt the mercy of her thoughts coming quickly, zooming through her head out the pen onto the paper. What a relief, she thought to herself; for a moment I thought I had dried up. She wrote a lot about what she felt, relishing the joy of her fingers gliding across the page, the sheer relief of communication. (241)

Not only does the "sheer relief of communication" enable Harriet to describe the events of the day, it allows her to "wr[i]te about what she felt" during these events, and reflect on their import. After watching curious people and curious activity in her community, she needs the white space of her notebook so she can unravel the "GREAT MYSTERY" of life (97). In fearing she had "dried up," Harriet equates her writing process to something as critical as water; without it, she may shrivel away. Alternatively, the text suggests here that to stay connected to the world of ideas, intellect, and artistic production, one must be continually, actively creating—*living* is creating. Whether these creations come in the form of Harriet's conclusions that her teacher must have a "TERRIBLE LIFE" because she saw her buy "ONE SMALL CAN OF TUNA, ONE DIET COLA, AND A PACK OF CIGARETTES" (33), or Wolfe's decoding of Ford Motors's attempt to control America through making teens think their car models are "boss," artifice and its processes exist as our only facts. As such, we must report them.

Harriet the Spy presents Harriet through multiple creative discourses: the third-person narrator, Harriet's notebook writing, and Harriet's writing for the Sixth Grade Page. Taken together, and in the context of New Journalism, these depictions show the instability of truth, fiction, and deception, and insinuate the difficulties traditional journalism has in conveying these nuances. After taking leadership of the Sixth Grade Page and printing her brutal anecdotes about Mrs. Plumber and Franca Dei Santi, Mrs. Welsch admonishes, "Harriet, you mustn't say such things" (289). However, Mr. Welsch wonders, "Why shouldn't she? It's the God's truth" (289). Mrs. Welsch does not respond, but the text does by implying that "the God's truth" is in the act of Harriet's writing. When Ole

Golly gives the controversial advice to Harriet that she must sometimes lie, the text equates lying to a creative act of artifice. Harriet must use her artistic capabilities to shape her writing according to its purpose. As such, by including different communicative modes, and by addressing the policing of knowledge by power structures, the novel recognizes its own construct and the slipperiness of labeling anything "God's truth"—except that of the process by which we arrive at individual comprehension of such a thing. The Sixth Grade Page, in its susceptibility to salacious gossip and eventual admission of lying, suggests the insufficiency (and potential danger) of traditional journalism alone.

The traditional newspaper, as depicted in the novel, enables the distribution of knowledge and the exposure of power structures, but when the reporter's process goes unacknowledged, the reporter risks replicating the same abuses of power that she hopes to unsettle. *Harriet the Spy* communicates the need to challenge social injustice, but questions the effectiveness of the disembodied voice, one that creates something ostensibly impersonal, but that is always somewhat personal. This larger cultural quandary filters through Harriet's editorship on the Sixth Grade Page via her inability to separate the purposes of private and public writing (which, in turn, forces consideration of what such distinctions should be). She uses the Sixth Grade Page to expose the power politics at play in Rachel Hawthorne's social club, from which she was ostracized. She includes the "very hot item" that "CERTAIN PEOPLE IN A CERTAIN CLUB OUGHT TO WATCH OUT" because other club members who "DON'T WANT TO SPEND ALL AFTERNOON DRINKING TEA" might stage a coup (291–92). Through both Harriet and Marion, we see a microcosm of American sociopolitical life and the role of the reporter. Marion seeks authority and control by creating a club in which she determines the members, or those with the right "attitude" (276). After spying on self-appointed President Marion and the activities of the club, Harriet perceives a corruption of power. Because Marion "IS GETTING TOO BIG FOR HER BRITCHES," muckraker Harriet sees fit for her "TO GET IT" through the exposure of her offenses (276). The text suggests that journalism be used more widely to expose corruption, but through Harriet's lack of editorial transparency it also intimates its problems of not specifying processes, limitations, and biases.

New Journalism and *Harriet the Spy* highlight the cultural significance of the investigative reporter who sees the world "afresh" and forthrightly acts as a creator, an artificer. Wolfe's New Journalists define their work through the quality not only of their reporting, but of their written craft. He aligns their work—intense observation and analysis of human events and conditions—with that of the great novelists, whom he deems reporters, too, saying we only have "to think of Balzac, Dickens, Gogol, Tolstoy, Dostoyevsky, and, in fact, Joyce.... It took the New Journalism to bring this strange matter of reporting to the foreground" ("New Journalism" 14). The novel shows Harriet in the process of finding her style; she "worked all day" on a story and then tries to experiment with imagery and rhetorical devices: "YESTERDAY I WENT INTO THAT HARDWARE STORE IT SMELLED LIKE THE INSIDE OF AN OLD THERMOS BOTTLE" (297). But Wolfe makes clear that while writers of New Journalism "were moving beyond the conventional limits of journalism," it was "not merely in terms of technique," but also their manner of reporting, one that "was more intense, more detailed, and certainly more time-consuming than anything that newspaper or magazine reporters, including investigative reporters, were accustomed to" ("New Journalism" 20–21). Wolfe implies that the work of the New Journalists encompasses something outside of fact, but truer than traditional journalism, and yet different from traditional fiction.

Critical to Harriet's assertion that she "want[s] to know everything" is the idea that she must find expression for her discoveries in order to ascertain truth. While her spoken desire to know everything stands as one of the essential passages in *Harriet the Spy*, another significant line follows this declaration. After Harriet's boisterous claim, Ole Golly tells her "It won't do you a bit of good to know everything if you don't do anything with it" (10). According to the novel, the young person possesses particular strength in engaging with and acting on the desire for knowledge. As such, it also suggests that adults grow irrelevant as they lose the grip of curiosity. *Harriet the Spy* ultimately equates curiosity *and* creativity with meaningful, active living and associates their loss with passive resignation. Children who maintain their curiosity and its expression throughout life become "people who love their work" and therefore "love life," while adults who "don't do anything" and "don't think anything" become "dull" (71, 57). Indeed, Harriet sees no end to her investigation into life, and she invites us to reassess how we understand boundaries of child and adult in contemporary American culture. "WHAT IS TOO OLD TO HAVE FUN?" she wonders, before deciding "YOU CAN'T BE TOO OLD TO SPY EXCEPT IF YOU WERE FIFTY YOU MIGHT FALL OFF A FIRE ESCAPE, BUT YOU COULD SPY AROUND ON THE GROUND A LOT" (57). In other words, age does not, or should not, deter the unending mission to know everything. In Harriet's world and according to the texts of New Journalism, we should all aspire to be spies. We are all reporters of life. We are all artificers.

The literary and historical dialogue explored throughout *Cub Reporters* raises questions regarding how American culture continues to redefine childhood, particularly its compulsion toward childhood containment. If the professionalization of journalism arguably depicts an attempt to more responsibly and accurately inform the public of national events, what larger story does the evolution of childhood tell us? Instead of maintaining the unrestrained freedom of moving about New York City—or any other large American city—directed by work, as the newsboy is, or for knowledge, as Harriet is, the ideal American child transitions into the comforts of confined spaces—home, school, adult supervision. More and more, we see the surrender of youthful independence and autonomy for something safe, secure, and unchallenging. *Harriet the Spy* and New Journalism offer innovative visions of both childhood and journalistic truth, but the spirit of those texts also implies that investigation and creative experimentation never end. The cub reporter, seeing things afresh, must continue to question how we confine ourselves through our constructs and underscore our ability to reconstruct, to reinvigorate. Such revelation, such liberation reminds us of the possibility for the fun in life—and really, "WHAT IS TOO OLD TO HAVE FUN?" We might further ask ourselves, "What is fun?" To return to *Hogan's Alley*'s Yellow Kid, fun is when we "git upon de stage an do our little turn" (Outcault Plate 28). Fun arises out of the exhilaration of discovery and creation, that which is new. And through our engagement with artifice, through our own cub reporting, life remains new—and fun.

NOTES

Introduction

1. "The Great Yellow Kid Newspaper War is supposed to have led the creation of the term 'yellow journalism' by traditional journalists, shocked and angered by the ignoble spectacle of two major newspapers slugging it out over a vulgar comic character," writes Bill Blackbeard (56). However, Blackbeard says that in actuality, "the phrase was first used in response to a national bicycle marathon sponsored by Hearst's California and New York newspapers" (56).

2. According to Frank Luther Mott, the "American newspaper . . . became 'big business'" by 1900 (*American Journalism* 546).

3. Anthony Fellow relates that "about 15" of these newspapers "were Tory organs" while the "others advocated the Patriot view" (59). In showing the critical role that publications played in forming national identity, as they were "valuable to each side in providing a unifying force and a platform for political conviction." Fellow also reminds us that "they obviously divided the country further by their unbridled partisanship" (59). As he puts it, "It may well be that the familiar saying 'You can't believe everything you read in the newspapers' had its roots in the press of the Revolution, when people believed only what was in the papers that represented their own political convictions" (59).

4. Mott goes on to say that newspapers of the early penny press period "required the spice of wit . . . the cayenne of a rather brutal human comedy. The penny press, said a magazine writer of the early fifties [1850s], 'answers the purpose of a pepper-box for diseased or slow stomachs, but it affords very little food for a healthy organization'" (*American Journalism* 242). Mott maintains that this assertion was "the general opinion of politicians, whose party organizations were flouted by the penny press; and of the professional and mercantile classes, whose institutions were commonly ignored or attacked" (*American Journalism* 242).

5. Barron further explains: "This campaign became but one side in a new culture war that began in the 1880s. But the genteel tradition's three core principles of character, virtue, and duty had always underpinned the genteels' publications. Such principles appeared in the very first American newspaper

published in the seventeenth century, and they continued to be heralded" (20).

6. Goodwin goes on to say that "McClure's formula—giving his writers the times and resources they needed to produce extended, intensively researched articles—was soon adopted by rival magazines" (xiii).

7. Canada relates that by 1850, newspapers were a common feature in both rural and urban American communities, with total circulation approximating five hundred million copies that year (31).

Chapter 1

1. Frank Luther Mott has written that the generations of men who solemnly and enthusiastically read Alger as boys "are apt to forget their author's banality, his typed characters, his bad writing, and his copybook moralities, and to remember only their boyish response to his getting-ahead thesis and their breathless interest in his rapid story-telling" (158). However, Mott adds, "Alger's name has become a by-word for the boy's success story, and that is no mean fame" (158). See Mott, *Golden Multitudes*.

2. The publication of Lewis Carroll's *Alice in Wonderland* (1865) generally marks the beginning of the Golden Age of children's literature. While the British *Alice* is viewed as quintessentially Victorian and serves as a source of national pride, it also changed the course of Western—and arguably global—children's literature as a whole by popularizing associations between childhood and curiosity.

3. In *A Connecticut Yankee in King Arthur's Court* (1889), Mark Twain imbues the cry of the newsboy not only with Americanness, but with a magical quality when protagonist Hank hears the sound for the first time since being transported to sixth-century England. After he manages to introduce the newspaper to Camelot, he tells us he soon heard

> a note that enchanted my soul and tumbled thirteen worthless centuries about my ears: "Camelot *Weekly Hosannah and Literary Volcano!*—latest irruption—only two cents—all about the big miracle in the Valley of Holiness!" One greater than kings had arrived—the newsboy. But I was the only person in all that throng who knew the meaning of this mighty birth, and what this imperial magician was come into the world to do. (245–46)

4. While there were instances of newsgirls, they were rare, and the public viewed them as somewhat shocking. Nasaw explains that although the

newspaper brass relentlessly pushed the newsboys' right to work in discussions surrounding child labors laws, they "surrendered when it came to girls" (103).

5. Further speaking to the value of the newsboy's role in American life is an 1887 newspaper article reprinted in the *Jackson Daily Citizen* (Jackson, MI). After describing France's newspaper vending machines, the writer declares that such a contraption could never function in the United States because of the essentiality of the physical newsboy, in both his presence and policies (which trump those of the "French newsboy" who does not give change or haggle). The writer implies that in the U.S. newsboy, we see a necessary reminder of the confident, bustling American spirit, for he "is the very embodiment of push and cheek. He hunts for buyers. . . . In stentorian voice he proclaims the most startling news in his papers" ("The French Newsboy" 6). Instead of being a passive worker merely waiting for customers, the American newsboy dedicates himself to disseminating news; armed with capitalistic curiosity, he "hunts" for potential newspaper readers. The "automaton can never replace our American newsboy," says the writer, though it may find its way into "our hotel lobbies" (6). The "elastic business methods" and cleverness of "our American newsboy will prevent this French invention from getting a foothold in this our glorious country" (6). Moreover, the writer imbues the American newsboy with a kind of superhuman quality as he describes him laboring, explaining that "he compels them [the public] to buy, and only relapses to the condition of a normal boy when his stack of papers has been disposed of" (6), thereby presenting an ideal or mythic example of economic and intellectual ingenuity to which "normal" children should aspire.

6. While late nineteenth-century American reporters received international praise, American newspaper publishers of the time stirred controversy. Any conversation about nineteenth-century American journalism must involve New York *World* publisher Joseph Pulitzer and his newspaper war with the *New York Journal*'s William Randolph Hearst, which arguably helped spur the Spanish American War of 1898. My argument contextualizes the broad progression of American journalism as seen through the newsboy, but it is important to point out this competition between these two men because newsboys became complicit in selling their schemes.

7. Though *Rough and Ready* repeatedly features Rufus "mak[ing] up a headline" as the reimagined *Newsies* do more than a century later, and notwithstanding the similarities we may find between Dick, Rufus, and the newsboy described in the 1854 *Gazette* article, contemporary reviewers of Alger noted the idealization with which he infused his early newsboys. Scharnhorst relates that

an 1869 *Rough and Ready* review published in the *Nation* "warned that Alger seemed bent upon self-parody and excoriated him for portraying newsboys as paragons of virtue" (*Lost Life* 89). In crafting a more-or-less righteous newsboy and despite Alger's assertion of reliance on real newsboys, Alger's novel illustrates an unbelievable newsboy, according to the *Nation*. The newsboy "'smokes ends of cigars which he picks up in the streets.... The newsboys who read 'Rough and Ready,' however they may approve it as a work of fiction, will say 'my eye' when asked to lay it to heart and make it a practical guide'" (qtd. in *Lost Life* 89). This passage exemplifies the problematic territory that the Alger legacy has created, in that there is a slippery relationship between Alger's writing, the rags-to-riches myth ascribed to his writing and inscribed into American consciousness, and the cultural reality of the second half of the century. But the *Nation* review, in suggesting that Alger produced an ideal vision of the newsboy unrecognizable from the lifestyle of real newsboys, hints that such a vision could serve as a "guide" (even though the writer is dubious about this).

8. Even before Ben starts selling newspapers, the cultural significance of journalism displays itself through the repeated references to newspapers and reporters, as well as the reporter-like behavior of Ben's friend Albert. Albert takes it upon himself to investigate Ben's stepfather, telling Ben, "I had a curiosity to find out what he was going to do, so I followed him.... There was a smaller tree near by, and I hid behind it so I could see what he was doing" (18). Albert reconnoiters and relays knowledge—reports—to Ben regarding where his stepfather may have hidden the family's (and his mother's) money. The novel deals in the acquisition of facts through self-instigated curiosity.

9. Snodgrass remarks to Ben that he has a perfect writer's name, given its alliterative quality. Given his own writer pseudonyms, such as Carl Cantab and Harry Hampton, Alger must have found such name-generating amusing.

10. When Snodgrass and Ben encounter a writer friend of Snodgrass's, the friend gives them this professional update: "'I have just sent one to the office of the *Weekly Tomahawk*. I would have sent it to the *Atlantic Monthly*, but that magazine is run by a clique, and no outsider stands any chance of getting in'" (99).

Chapter 2

1. Davis's *Harper's Weekly* articles about this trip were collectively published in *The West from a Car-Window* (1892). The opening sentences of the book capture a certain ambivalence about the journey, both poignant and perhaps surprising coming from Davis, whose reputation for adventure and travel

predominates his legacy. He admits that the first leg of the trip is "somewhat disturbing to one who visits the West for the first time with the purpose of writing of it" because of the area's vastness (8). "It gives him a sharp sensation of loneliness," Davis confesses, "a wish to apologize to some one [sic], and he is moved with a sudden desire to get out at the first station and take the next train back, before his presumption is discovered" (8).

2. Davis wrote to his mother in 1890 to recount a meeting he had with Alden, telling her, "[T]he advice, offers and encouragement he gave me were worth hundreds of dollars." During their conversation, explains Davis in the letter, Alden said that Davis's stories expressed "'light in a grand and noble way. It shows the power to feel and to stand apart and touch these feelings deliberately. We have had no such a writer in this country. The French have them but America has wanted one for years and you are the man'" (Undated Letter to Mother, 1890).

3. Amy Kaplan reads *Soldiers of Fortune* as a "historical romance" that "remaps a new world out of the ruins of a decayed empire and a thwarted revolution," thus demonstrating how the "American hero can best prove his masculinity outside his national boundaries" (670–71), and argues that the novel and other romances of the period fueled the jingoistic fervor leading into the Spanish-American War.

4. Greta D. Little, meanwhile, sees an implicit theme of curiosity developing in American children's literature as early as the beginning of the nineteenth century, with "[y]oungsters finally beg[inning] to appear as living, breathing individuals," a move away from the "themes" of "obedience, submissiveness, and satisfaction with one's place in life" found in earlier literature (188). Little further explains that "[a]s the nineteenth century opened, the reforms suggested by Rousseau and the reformers who followed him opened the way for natural, spontaneous learning through experience, creating a place for curiosity" (188).

5. Anne Dhu Shapiro relates that the "first explicitly musical theater in the eighteenth-century colonies of North America was not ballad opera, but pantomime" (50). The form "was to continue as a favorite type of entertainment in the colonies throughout the eighteenth century and well into the nineteenth, when it coalesced with French ballet, the circus, or theatrical extravaganza" (50). See Shapiro, 49–72.

6. In a 1925 piece for the *North American Review*, Montrose J. Moses asserts that the boy reader "demands an up-to-dateness his father requires in the morning paper. That is why boys' stories are reportorial" (10). However, Moses does not further expand on his exact meaning of "reportorial" or its implications in terms of children's literature.

7. After the initial publication of *Gallegher and Other Stories*, Davis wrote the following in a May 21 letter to his family: "Scribner has issued the second edition of Gallegher and says a third maybe expected very soon 4000 copies have been printed in both editions. That is not large but it will do." (The year, by all accounts, should be 1891 or 1892, though the letter was catalogued in a folder labeled 1890.) Davis subsequently wrote to tell of the book's translation into French and German (Letter to Family, May 21; Undated Letters to Family).

8. Concerning the concept of intuition, Emerson writes,

> The magnetism which all original action exerts is explained when we inquire the reason of self-trust. Who is the Trustee? What is the aboriginal Self on which a universal reliance may be grounded? What is the nature and power of that science-baffling star, without parallax, without calculable elements, which shoots a ray of beauty even into trivial and impure actions, if the least mark of independence appear? The inquiry leads us to that source, at once the essence of genius, of virtue, and of life, which we call Spontaneity or Instinct. We denote this primary wisdom as Intuition, whilst all later teachings are tuitions. (See Emerson, 127)

9. Such debate came into sharp focus in 1904 after Horace White argued against Joseph Pulitzer's proposal in the pages of the *North American Review*. Shortly thereafter, the magazine printed Pulitzer's defense of such a school.

10. "Gallegher" also condemns adults for their preoccupation with vice as opposed to more productive pursuits: "There was a great deal of betting, and all of the men handled the great roll of bills they wagered with a flippant recklessness which could only be accounted for in Gallegher's mind by temporary mental derangement" (29).

11. The title is taken from Rudyard Kipling's novella *The Man Who Would Be King* (1888). Davis greatly admired Kipling's work. He wrote to his mother in late May of 1890 to say that he had "been reading Rudyard Kipling's short stories" and found it "disgusting that a boy like that should write such stories. He has not left himself anything to do when he gets old" (Letter to Mother Dated "late May").

12. Other titles in *Stories for Boys* include "Midsummer Pirates," "The Great Tri-Club Tennis Tournament," and "The Van Bibber Baseball Club."

13. Gordon decides that the Bradleys "ought to act as a guard of honor" and gives "them each a pair of the captain's rejected white duck trousers, and a blue jersey apiece, with a big white Y on it" (24).

14. In this, the story presages an alleged episode involving William Randolph Hearst. "Perhaps the myth told most often about yellow journalism,"

writes W. Joseph Campbell, "is that of the purported exchange of telegrams between Hearst and the artist Frederic Remington, in which Hearst is said to have vowed, 'I'll furnish the war,' between the United States and Spain" (2).

15. Today we associate yellow journalism with that of the salient, shocking, and specious, but what it was and was not remains a contested subject. Arthur Brisbane, Davis's friend and an editor for William Randolph Hearst's *New York Journal*, once said, "Anything in journalism that is new and successful is yellow journalism, no matter what you or I see fit to call it" (qtd. in Campbell 6). W. Joseph Campbell argues that rather than being "an entertainment medium . . . that frivolously discounted and even corrupted, fact-based journalism," yellow journalism helped improve and sophisticate reporting. One of the "defining characteristic[s] of the yellow press—and, notably, of Hearst's *Journal*," Campbell writes, "was abundant spending on newsgathering, especially on news from afar" (2).

16. Davis also noted the Hearst's expenditures, detailing his payment of $3,000 for a month's work and his purchase of items at the *Journal*'s expense, including "a fifty dollar field glass which is a new invention and the best made" (Letter to Mother, Dec. 19, 1896). "Maybe I don't spend all of 'Willie' Hearst's money as it is," he later commented to his mother. "I burn it" (Letter to Mother, Jan. 16, 1897).

17. The grand illusions of war fade for Davis during his time in Cuba, and he begins to see it for the political, financial production it is: "If this is war I am of the opinion that it is a senseless wicked institution made for soldiers, lovers, and correspondents for different reasons, and for no one else in the world and its [sic] too expensive for the others to keep it going to entertain these few gentlemen" (Letter to Mother, Jan. 16, 1897).

18. Phrases such as "yellow kid reporters" and yellow journalism began with the circulation battle between Hearst and Pulitzer in the late 1890s, when each ran a version of the popular comic that the *Sun* called the "Yellow Kid." Campbell further relates

> Many media historians credit Ervin Wardman, the stern-looking editor of the long-defunct *New York Press*, for having coined the term [yellow journalism], presumably in late 1896. According to the most common version of the etiology of the phrase, Wardman derived "yellow journalism" to characterize the rivalry between William Randolph Hearst and Joseph Pulitzer, particularly in their contest for the services of R. F. Outcault. Outcault was the artist who drew a witty and colorful cartoon that depicted the antics and

the friends of the Yellow Kid, an irreverent, jug-eared child of the New York City tenements. (25)

19. A letter Davis sent to Rebecca on the matter reads

And since the Journal published the page of stuff saying I was with the insurgents I fear my usefulness is ended—they lost the best story in Cuba by that act which was intended to "force"... me to do what they said I was doing—it just boomeranged them and will and has queered me. (Letter to Mother, Jan. 24, 1897, from Siego de Avila)

Chapter 3

1. In fact, the first issue of the *Pioneer* coincided with the day of Nellie Bly's return to New York City and *The World* office on Jan. 25, 1890 (Rogers 25; Kroeger 172).

2. Various websites, for example, erroneously cite Bly's "hot air balloon journey" as one of her many feats, in the manner that the New York City Department of Parks and Recreation does on their page for Nellie Bly Park in Brooklyn ("Nellie Bly Park" n. p.).

3. Because of the racial and economic barriers of the period and the nature of the stories being told during this time, the texts and histories considered in this chapter refer to girls and young women who are presumably white and middle to upper class. However, the incredible journalistic work during the late nineteenth century and early twentieth century of minority women should not be overlooked. Specifically, Ida B. Wells's writings and activism showed the need for uncompromising journalism in the face of oppression and dehumanization, exposing acts of atrocity such as the lynching of African Americans.

4. Kenneth Burke explains that "among what he called the six qualitative parts of tragedy (plot, character, thought, diction, melody, and spectacle)" Aristotle "rated spectacle (*opsis*) lowest—whereas the high development of technology today readily allows for kinds of 'spectacular' in which the visual show is the major source of attraction." See Burke, 298.

5. Green writes that Pulitzer also "rallied New Yorkers to contribute $100,000 worth of pennies to give the Statue of Liberty a proper pedestal" while "Hearst tried to lure readers to an archeological discovery with the headline 'Most Colossal Animal Ever on Earth Just Found Out West,' making it sound like a brontosaurus might still be roaming the earth" (42).

6. Scharnhorst describes the "vexed relationship" between Field and Samuel Clemens, who both worked as correspondents and columnists for various newspapers in the late nineteenth century (194). "Clemens's attitude toward Field,"

writes Scharnhorst, "was consistently that of a Victorian patriarch. He treated her with undisguised condescension both privately and publicly, in both his own voice and anonymously" (195).

7. Jean Marie Lutes helpfully reminds us, "For men, participatory journalism"—stunt reporting—"was a choice; for women, it was one of the few ways to break out of the women's pages" (2).

8. As an immigrant himself, Pulitzer recognized the significance of reaching out to marginalized segments of society. Brooke Kroeger tells of how he used this awareness as part of his shrewd approach to the *World*'s newspaper coverage, affirming that he "instinctively understood the need to appeal to the diverse pool of potential readership presented by the masses of new Americans settling in the city" (80). Pulitzer "took up their causes, appealed to their interests, confronted in newsprint the issues they faced, and commanded their attention" (80).

9. Biographer Katherine Rogers relates Baum's anger when he learned that his publishers changed the novel's original *Aunt Jane's Nieces in Journalism* title to *Aunt Jane's Nieces on Vacation*, suggesting that importance Baum attached to having the word "journalism" in the book's name (279).

Chapter 4

1. Violet Harris recounts the frequent stereotypes children came across in popular literature of the late nineteenth century, such as the mammy character of Aunt Chloe in *Elsie Dinsmore* (1867) and the "comic Negro" figure, generally "African American males . . . depicted as dimwitted children who constantly grin, eat, misunderstand simple directions, and scratch their heads" (542).

2. Though *The Brownies' Book* lasted only two years, its revolutionary mission of creating a literary and cultural space expressly for black children provided the groundwork for the Defender Junior and later children's literature that focused on engaging an African American audience, such as *Popo and Fifina: Children of Haiti* (1932) by Arno Bontemps and Langston Hughes. The emphasis on the production of a print periodical, because of its necessary negotiation of authors, content, and overall vision, make community and collaboration crucial themes in the development of African American children's literature during the Harlem Renaissance. Additionally, the scarcity of literature for black children (or literature with positive representations of black children) in early twentieth-century America extended to popular children's periodicals. The generally well-regarded *St. Nicholas Magazine* "either ignored the existence of African Americans or, worse, depicted them in a stereotypical and dehumanizing manner," argues Jonda C. McNair (5). She further contends, "Stories that ridiculed African Americans

were commonplace in the magazine" (5). In this light, we can better see why scholars consider *The Brownies' Book* a substantial contribution to African American literature and children's literature in general. *The Brownies' Book* "laid the foundation for a new tradition in children's literature," McNair asserts, "a tradition that challenged the stereotypical depictions of African Americans in mainstream children's literature" (6).

3. "The emulation of white cultural models embedded in configurations of uplift frequently conflicted with the era's ethos of cultural nationalism," Smith writes, "producing compelling ambiguities and ambivalences within the children's texts that aimed to develop race activists" (xvii).

4. In the 1934 text *Race Relations*, civil rights advocates Willis D. Weatherford and Charles S. Johnson write: "'Negro papers are first of all race papers. They are first and foremost interested in the advancement of the race'" (qtd. in Myrdal 908).

5. "The *Defender* fed its public red-ink sensationalism," according to Ottley, "and when pushed for the reason, Abbott had the identical defense his white colleagues offered: he wanted to reach the largest possible number of readers, in order to use that following as an instrument for improving and advancing the race" (131). In other words, "sensationalism seemed to him a rational policy" to achieve these ends (Ottley 131).

6. Chicago newspaperman, poet, and children's writer Carl Sandburg once wrote in a 1919 *Chicago Daily News* article that "'more than any other one agency,'" the *Defender* "'was the big cause of the 'northern fever' and the big exodus from the south'" (qtd. in Ottley 159).

7. Grossman, describing the sensational tendencies of the newspaper, writes, "In reporting news of white violence against blacks in the South, *Defender* correspondents spared few of the gory details, and the editors reputedly embellished them even further" (75).

8. McClary outlines a recurrent scene from her childhood that would happen after the post arrived. The lucky young mail recipient would boast something along the lines of, "'Hey guess what, I got a letter addressed to me today. And guess what was in it. Naw, girl, I know you'll never guess, so I'll just show you—LOOK'" (56). Then, "the pin was thrust out to get the admiring glances it deserved," McClary says (56).

9. The first appearance of the Defender Junior in the digital archives of the *Chicago Defender* is April 2, 1921. Other publications have erroneously reported 1923 as the start date. In a column recalling how he came up with the idea for the section, Harper cites 1919 as the year when a young boy from "Indiana ave." gave him a poem to publish, which contributed to Harper launching

the Defender Junior. The first column featured the poem of that young boy, Sidney Poole. It is unclear whether Harper misremembers the date, or whether there was a two-year gap between when he was given the poem and when the first Defender Junior section was actually printed in the pages of the *Defender* (Harper 1, 6).

10. Mercer's poem reads:

C stands for Charity—a noble cause.
H stands for Harmony, towards one and all.
I stands for Infinite—her future grand.
C stands for character—her eminent stand.
A stands for August, her illustrious staff.
G stands for Grandeur: she stands no gaff.
O stands for Omnipotent—she is feared by the mass.
D stands for Dauntless: she is fearless and brave.
E stands for Eternal, forever she will save.
F stands for Fraterniay [sic], a brother to all.
E stands for Edifice, to humany [sic] it calls.
N stands for the Nation, of which she is a part.
D stands for Diplomacy, she enters the heart.
E stands for Efficacy, the power to succeed.
R stands for Right or Righteousness, of which we all need.
("Chicago Defender Junior," Nov. 15, 1924, A3)

Conclusion

1. Jerry Griswold reminds us that in the late nineteenth century, "an interest in Children's Literature by all kinds of authors was not uncommon then; the ghettoization of children's writers is a relatively modern phenomenon" (19). *Harriet the Spy*, as such, does not enjoy the same critical acclaim or attention that the works of Mark Twain, for instance, receive from scholars outside children's literature studies.

2. Anita Silvey, a former children's publishing editor, explains to Grant that "'*Harriet the Spy* was controversial when it came out in the 60s . . . in part because Harriet was a very flawed character. Some critics hated the book, and some schools even banned it. Harriet saw too much, said too much'" (Grant).

3. "'Children,'" Viguers argues, "do not enjoy cynicism. I doubt its appeal to many of them. This is a very jaded view on which to open children's windows'" (qtd. in Bernstein 833). According to Bernstein, after Viguers's article, "three

main criticisms emerged [among librarians and educators]: the characters were too unpleasant, children might imitate Harriet's spying, and Ole Golly's final advice [that sometimes we must lie] was immoral" (Bernstein 833). In reaction to the controversy surrounding *Harriet the Spy*, "[m]any libraries established special committees to decide whether or not the book deserved space on the shelves" (833). Bernstein points out that "[a]lthough generally recognized today as a masterpiece of children's literature, the book has won only one award: the 1967 Sequoyah Award, given each year by children in Oklahoma" (833). As such, "[n]o adults have ever formally honoured the book" (833).

4. Kevin Kerrane points out that the term "new journalism" rebrands a former iteration used in the late nineteenth and early twentieth centuries:

> The term "new journalism," in fact, was originally coined by Matthew Arnold in 1887 to describe the style of Stead's *Pall Mall Gazette*: brash, vivid, personal, reform-minded—and occasionally, from Arnold's conservative viewpoint, "featherbrained." The Victorian social reporters, and the American muckrakers who followed them, aimed at a factual literature of modern industrial life. Their literary touches came less from artistic design than from the writer' sense of moral or political urgency: a determination to dramatize the reality of poverty, prostitution, and prejudice. (17)

5. Wolfe further outlines a growing feeling of ennui among some journalists in terms of approach, and the collective impulse toward a radical change:

> In the mid-1960s that was exactly the feeling I had. I'm sure that others who were experimenting with magazine articles, such as [Gay] Talese, began to feel the same way. They were moving beyond the conventional limits of journalism, but not merely in terms of technique. The kind of reporting they were doing struck them as far more ambitious, too. It was more intense, more detailed, and certainly more time-consuming than anything that newspaper or magazine reporters, including investigative reporters, were accustomed to. ("New Journalism" 20–21)

6. In an introductory note to this scene, Wolfe says, "There was an unusually rich record of Kesey's thoughts and feelings during this interlude. He had written at length to his friend Larry McMurtry about it at the time, he had made tapes even while he was in the jungle, and I had interviewed his companions in flight, Zonker and Black Maria, about it, as well as Kesey himself, of course" (*The Electric Kool-Aid Acid Test* 204). "Much of the direct interior monologue is taken from Kesey's letters to McMurtry," he explains (204).

WORKS CITED

"Abbott-Sengstacke Family Papers." *Chicago Public Library.* Chicago Public Library, n.d. Web. 10 March 2015.

Alger, Horatio, Jr. "Are My Boys Real?" *Ragged Dick; or, Street Life in New York with Boot Blacks.* By Horatio Alger, Jr., edited by Hildegard Hoeller. Norton Critical Edition. New York: Norton, 2008, 122—24. Print.

——. *Ben Bruce: Scenes in the Life of a Bowery Newsboy.* 1892. New York: A. L. Burt, 1901. De Grummond Children's Literature Collection. Print.

——. *Dan, the Newsboy.* New York: A. L. Burt, 1893. *Archive.org.* Web. 20 Oct. 2012.

——. *Luke Walton; or the Chicago Newsboy.* 1889. Chicago: M. A. Donohue, 1905. Print.

——. *Fame and Fortune, or, The Progress of Richard Hunter.* Boston: A. K. Loring, 1868. *Archive.org.* Web. 18 July 2014.

——. *Ragged Dick; or, Street Life in New York with Boot Blacks,* edited by Hildegard Hoeller. Norton Critical Edition. New York: Norton, 2008. Print.

——. *Rough and Ready; or Life among the New York Newsboys.* 1869. Racine, WI: Whitman Publishing, n.d. Print.

——. *The Telegraph Boy.* New York: A. L. Burt, 1887. *Archive.org.* Web. 22 Feb. 2014.

Anderson, Benedict. "From Imagined Communities: Reflections on the Origin and Spread of Nationalism." *Theory of the Novel: A Historical Approach,* edited by Michael McKeon. Baltimore: Johns Hopkins UP, 2000, 414–34. Print.

Anatol, Giselle Liza. "Children's and Young Adult Literatures." *The Cambridge History of African American Literature,* edited by Maryemma Graham and Jerry W. Ward, Jr. Cambridge, UK: Cambridge UP, 2011, 621–54. Print.

"artifice, n." *OED Online.* Oxford University Press, December 2015. Web. 26 February 2016.

Avery, Gillian. *Behold the Child: American Children and Their Books 1621–1922.* London: Random House, 1994. Print.

Bakhtin, Mikhail. *Problems of Dostoevsky's Poetics, edited and* translated by Caryl Emerson. Minneapolis: U of Minnesota P, 1984. Print.

"Banner for the Chicago Defender Jr." *Chicago Defender* 29 Apr 1922: 14. *ProQuest Historical Newspapers.* Web. 28 Feb. 2015.

Banning, Stephen A. "The Professionalization of Journalism" *Journalism History* 24:4 (Winter 1998): 157–63.

Barron, Jonathan. *How Robert Frost Made Realism Matter*. Columbia: University of Missouri Press, 2015. Print.

Barthes, Roland. "Introduction to the Structural Analysis of Narratives." *Image, Music, Text*, translated by Stephen Heath. New York: Hill and Wang (Farrar, Straus and Giroux), 1977. 79–124. Print.

Bartow, Edith Merwin. *News and These United States*. New York: Funk & Wagnalls, 1952. Print.

Baum, L. Frank. *The Annotated Wizard of Oz*, edited by Michael Patrick Hearn. New York: Norton, 2000. Print.

———. *Our Landlady*, edited by Nancy Tystad Koupal. Lincoln: U of Nebraska P, 1996. Print.

———. "What Children Want." *Baum's Road to Oz: The Dakota Years* edited by Nancy Tystad Koupal. Pierre: South Dakota State Historical Society P, 2000. 166–70. Print.

———(under Edith Van Dyne). *Aunt Jane's Nieces*. Chicago: Reilly & Britton, 1906. *Google Books*. Web. 19 Jan. 2014.

———(under Edith Van Dyne). *Aunt Jane's Nieces on Vacation*. Chicago: Reilly & Britton, 1912.

Beasley, Maurine H., and Sheila J. Gibbons. *Taking Their Place: A Documentary History of Women and Journalism*. Washington, DC: American University Press, 1993.

bebesadie. "Mattie Rehearsing 'Carrying the Banner' from *Newsies*." *YouTube*. 2 April 2014. Web. 1 July 2014.

Benton, Mike. *The Comic Book in America: An Illustrated History*. Dallas: Taylor Publishing, 1989. Print.

Bernstein, Robin. "Louise Fitzhugh." *Censorship: A World Encyclopedia*, edited by Derek Jones. London: Routledge, 2001 832–833. *Google Books*. Web. 13 Jan. 2016.

———. *Racial Innocence: Performing American Childhood from Slavery to Civil Rights*. New York: NYU Press, 2011. Print.

"A Bibliography of Horatio Alger, Jr. Related Materials in Print." University Libraries' Rare Books & Special Collections at Northern Illinois University. Web. 1 June 2014.

Black, Lisa, Deanese Williams-Harris, and Carlos Sadovi. "Shooting Near Bud Billiken Parade: 'I Am Tired of This.'" *ChicagoTribune.com*. 9 Aug. 2014. Web. 4 March 2015.

Blackbeard, Bill. *R. F. Outcault's The Yellow Kid: A Centennial Celebration of the Kid Who Started the Comics*. Northampton, MA: Kitchen Sink Press, 1995. Print.

"BREAKING NEWS: NEWSIES to Close on Broadway This August." *Broadwayworld.com*. Wisdom Digital Media. 22 June 2014. Web. 1 July 2014.

Brecht, Bertolt. *Brecht on Theatre*, translated by John Willett. New York: Farrar, Straus, and Giroux/Hill and Wang, 1964. Print.

"Bud Billiken Club Membership Form." *Chicago Defender* 29 Apr. 1922: 14. *ProQuest Historical Newspapers*. Web. 28 Feb. 2015.

Burke, Kenneth. "Why *A Midsummer Night's Dream*?" *Shakespeare Quarterly* 57:3 (2006): 297–308. *JSTOR*. Web. 9 March 2016.

Campbell, W. Joseph. *Yellow Journalism: Puncturing the Myths, Defining the Legacies*. Westport, CT: Praeger Publishers, 2001.

Canada, Mark. *Literature and Journalism in Antebellum America: Thoreau, Stowe, and Their Contemporaries Respond to the Rise of the Commercial Press*. New York: Palgrave Macmillan, 2011. Print.

Carey, James W. "The Problems of Journalism History." *The American Journalism History Reader: Critical and Primary Texts*, edited by Bonnie Brennen and Hanno Hardt. New York: Routledge, 2011. 22–27. Print.

Carpenter, Humphrey, and Mari Prichard. *The Oxford Companion to Children's Literature*. Oxford, UK: Oxford University Press, 1984. Print.

"Chicago Defender Junior: For Young Folks Help Me Out, Please." *Chicago Defender* 2 April 1921: 5. *ProQuest Historical Newspapers*. Web. 11 Feb. 2015.

"Chicago Defender Junior: For Young Folks By Young Tolks [sic] Let's Do Something." *Chicago Defender* 23 April 1921: 5. *ProQuest Historical Newspapers*. Web. 11 Feb. 2015.

"Chicago Defender Junior: For Young Folks By Young Folks." *Chicago Defender* 11 June 1921: 8. *ProQuest Historical Newspapers*. Web. 15 Feb. 2015.

"Chicago Defender Junior: FOR YOUNG FOLKS BY YOUNG FOLKS." *Chicago Defender* 25 June 1921: 8. *ProQuest Historical Newspapers*. Web. 15 Feb. 2015.

"Chicago Defender Junior: For Young Folks By Young Folks." *Chicago Defender* 2 July 1921: 6. *ProQuest Historical Newspapers*. Web. 21 Feb. 2015.

"The City Newsboys Are a Peculiar Class of our Local Population, and Attract No Small Share of the Attention of Strangers from the Interior." *North American and United States Gazette* (Philadelphia, PA). 15 September 1854: Issue 19,198; col. B. *19th Century U.S. Newspapers*. Web. 11 Oct. 2012.

Clark, Beverly Lyon. *Kiddie Lit: The Cultural Construction of Children's Literature in America*. Baltimore: Johns Hopkins UP, 2003. Print.

Connery, Thomas B. *Journalism and Realism: Rendering American Life*. Evanston, IL: Northwestern UP, 2011. Print.

Dana, Charles A. *The Art of Newspaper Making: Three Lectures*. 1895. New York: Arno Press, 1970. Print.

Davis, Rebecca Harding. 1871 Undated Diary Pieces. Box 1. Folder 1865–1879. Richard Harding Davis Collection (#6109). Albert and Shirley Small Special Collections Library. University of Virginia, Charlottesville. 4 Aug. 2014.

Davis, Richard Harding. *Gallegher and Other Stories*. New York: Charles Scribner's Sons, 1891. Print.

———. Letter to Mother, March 11, 1893. Box 3. Folder 1893 Jan.–Mar. Richard Harding Davis Collection (#6109). Albert and Shirley Small Special Collections Library. University of Virginia, Charlottesville. 14 Aug. 2014.

———. Letter to Mother Dated "Late May." Box 2. Folder 1890 Apr.–Oct. Richard Harding Davis Collection (#6109). Albert and Shirley Small Special Collections Library. University of Virginia, Charlottesville. Aug. 7, 2014.

———. Undated Letter to Mother, 1890. Box 2. Folder 1890, n.d. Richard Harding Davis Collection (#6109). Albert and Shirley Small Special Collections Library. University of Virginia, Charlottesville. 7 Aug. 2014.

———. Letter to Family. Box 2. May 21 [1891 or 1892?]. Folder 1890 Apr.–Oct. Richard Harding Davis Collection (#6109). Albert and Shirley Small Special Collections Library. University of Virginia, Charlottesville. 8 Aug. 2014.

———. Undated Letters to Family [1891 or 1892?]. Box 2. Folder 1890 (n.d.). Richard Harding Davis Collection (#6109). Albert and Shirley Small Special Collections Library. University of Virginia, Charlottesville. 9 Aug. 2014.

———. Undated Letter to Mother, 1889. Box 2. Folder 1889. Richard Harding Davis Collection (#6109). Albert and Shirley Small Special Collections Library. University of Virginia, Charlottesville. 8 Aug. 2014.

———. Letter to Mother, Dec. 19, 1896. Box 3. Folder 1896 Dec.–n.d. Richard Harding Davis Collection (#6109). Albert and Shirley Small Special Collections Library. University of Virginia, Charlottesville. 11 Dec. 2014.

———. Letter to Mother, Jan. 4, 1897, from Key West. Box 4. Folder 1897 Jan.–Dec. Richard Harding Davis Collection (#6109). Albert and Shirley Small Special Collections Library. University of Virginia, Charlottesville. 14 Dec. 2014.

———. Letter to Mother, Jan. 16, 1897 from Cardenas–North Coast of Cuba. Box 4. Folder 1897. Richard Harding Davis Collection (#6109). Albert and Shirley Small Special Collections Library. University of Virginia, Charlottesville. 14 Dec. 2014.

———. Letter to Mother, Jan. 24, 1897, from Siego de Avilla. Box 4. Folder 1897. Richard Harding Davis Collection (#6109). Albert and Shirley Small Special Collections Library. University of Virginia. Charlottesville, VA. 15 Dec. 2014.

———. *Stories for Boys*. 1891. New York: Charles Scribner's Sons, 1896. *Internet Archive*. University of California. Web. 22 Aug. 2014.

———. *The West from a Car-Window*. 1892. New York: Harper & Brothers. *Internet Archive*. University of Michigan. Web. 7 Sept. 2014.

"The Defender Junior: School Study Sports Home Play Work Applications." *Chicago Defender* 14 Jan. 1922: 18. *ProQuest Historical Newspapers*. Web. 23 Feb. 2015.

"The Defender Junior Children's Greatest Newspaper: School Study Sports Home Play Work Applications." *Chicago Defender* 4 Feb. 1922: A2. *ProQuest Historical Newspapers*. Web. 25 Feb. 2015.

"The Defender Junior Children's Greatest Newspaper: School Study Sports Home Play Work Bud Says." *Chicago Defender* 29 Apr. 1922: 14. *ProQuest Historical Newspapers*. Web. 28 Feb. 2015.

"The Defender Junior Children's Greatest Newspaper: School Study Sports Home Play Work." *Chicago Defender* 15 Nov. 1924: A3. *ProQuest Historical Newspapers*. Web. 26 Feb. 2015.

DiGirolamo, Vincent. "The Black Newsboy: Black Child in a White Myth." *Columbia Journal of American Studies* 4:1 (2000): 63–92. Print.

"Do You Want To Be a Reporter?" *Augusta Chronicle* (Augusta, GA) 25 Aug. 1902: 5. *American's Historical Newspapers*. Web. 19 Oct. 2014.

Douglas, George H. *The Golden Age of the Newspaper*. Westport, CT: Greenwood Press, 1999. Print.

Duane, Anne Mae. "Introduction." *The Children's Table: Childhood Studies and the Humanities*, edited by Anna Mae Duane. Athens: University of Georgia Press, 2014. 1–14. Print.

Du Bois, W. E. B., ed. *The Brownies' Book*. 1920–21. Rare Book and Special Collections Division. Library of Congress. Web. 15 Feb 2014.

Edelstein, Sari. *Between the Novel and the News: The Emergence of American Women's Writing*. Charlottesville: University of Virginia Press, 2014.

Emerson, Ralph Waldo. "Self-Reliance." *Emerson's Prose and Poetry*, edited by Joel Porte and Saundra Morris. 120–136. New York: Norton, 2001. Print.

Emery, Edwin. *The Press and America: An Interpretive History of Mass Media.* Englewood Cliffs, NJ: Prentice-Hall, 1972. Print.

"Evolution of the Newsboy. Holding His End up, in His Way, as Well as Anybody." The Sunday State (Charleston, SC). 11 Nov. 1900: 4. *America's Historical Newspapers.* Web. 1 Nov. 2012.

Fahs, Alice. *Out on Assignment: Newspaper Women and the Making of the Modern Public Space.* Chapel Hill: U of North Carolina P, 2011. Print.

Feldman, Jack, and Alan Menken. "Carrying the Banner." *Newsies: The Musical.* Ghostlight Records, 2012. CD.

———. "The World Will Know." *Newsies: The Musical.* Ghostlight Records, 2012. CD.

Fellow, Anthony R. *American Media History.* 3rd ed. Boston: Wadsworth, 2013. Print.

Fishkin, Shelley Fisher. *From Fact to Fiction: Journalism and Imaginative Writing in America.* Baltimore: John Hopkins UP, 1985. Print.

Fitzhugh, Louise. *Harriet the Spy.* 1964. New York: Yearling, 1992. Print.

"A French Newsboy. An Automatic Vendor of Daily Papers." *Jackson Daily Citizen* (Jackson, MI) 28 May 1887: 6. *America's Historical Newspapers.* Web. 27 Feb. 2014.

Gage, Matilda Joslyn. *Woman, Church and State.* 1893. New York: Arno Press. 1972. Print.

Gallagher, Catherine, and Stephen Greenblatt. *Practicing New Historicism.* Chicago: U of Chicago P, 2000. Print.

Grant, Neva. "Unapologetically Harriet, the Misfit Spy." NPR.org. 3 March 2008. Web. 10 Jan. 2016.

Gibson, Charles Dana. "The First Glimpse of Davis." *R. H. D.: Appreciations of Richard Harding Davis.* New York: Charles Scribner's Sons, 1917. 29–32. Print.

"Girl Reporter Plays Fly." *The Seattle Star* Nov. 5, 1915: 1. *Chronicling America.* Library of Congress. Web. 20 Jan 2015.

"Girls Edit Paper. Oregon University Co-Eds to Show Men Few Tricks." *The Oregonian (The Morning Oregonian;* Portland, Oregon). 21 May 1910: 6. *America's Historical Newspapers.* Web. 26 Oct. 2014.

Goodwin, Doris Kearns. *The Bully Pulpit: Theodore Roosevelt, William Howard Taft and the Golden Age of Journalism.* New York: Simon and Schuster, 2013. *Google Books.* Web. 23 July 2014.

Green, Norma. "Concepts of News." *American Journalism: History, Principles, Practices,* edited by W. David Sloan and Lisa Mullikin Parcell. Jefferson, NC: McFarland, 2002. 34–42. Print.

Griswold, Jerry. *Audacious Kids: Coming of Age in America's Classic Children's Books*. New York: Oxford UP, 1992. Print.
Grossman, James R. *Land of Hope: Chicago, Black Southerners, and the Great Migration*. Chicago: U of Chicago P, 1989. Print.
Gubar, Marah. *Artful Dodgers: Reconceiving the Golden Age of Children's Literature*. Oxford: Oxford UP, 2009. Print.
Foucault, Michel. *Politics, Philosophy, Culture: Interviews and Other Writings, 1977–1984*. New York: Routledge, 1988. *Google Books*. Web. 26 March 2014.
Harper, Lucius C. "Dustin' off the News: This Sad-Eyed, Soft-Spoken Boy Became Famous." *Chicago Defender* 25 Aug. 1947:1, 6. *ProQuest Historical Newspapers*. Web. 21 March 2015.
Harris, Violet J. "African American Children's Literature: The First One Hundred Years." *Journal of Negro Education* 59:4 (1990): 540–55. *JSTOR*. Web. 11 April 2015.
Hawthorne, Nathaniel. *The House of the Seven Gables*. Cutchogue, NY: Buccaneer Books, 1987. Print.
Hellmann, John. "Fables of Fact: New Journalism Reconsidered." *The Centennial Review* 21:4 (1977): 414–32. *JSTOR*. Web. 13 Jan. 2016.
Hendler, Glenn. "Pandering in the Public Sphere: Masculinity and the Market in Horatio Alger." *American Quarterly* 48:3 (1996): 415–38. *Project Muse*. Web. 24 Oct. 2012.
Horkheimer, Max, and Theodor W. Adorno. *Dialectic of Enlightenment*, translated by John Cumming. New York: Continuum, 1988. Print.
Johnson-Feelings, Dianne. "Preface." *The Best of the Brownies' Book*, edited by Dianne Johnson-Feelings. 12–15. New York: Oxford UP, 1996. Print.
Kaplan, Amy. "Romancing the Empire: The Embodiment of American Masculinity in the Popular Historical Novel of the 1890s." *American Literary History* 2:4 (1990): 659–90. *JSTOR*. Web. 1 Sept. 2014.
———. *The Social Construction of American Realism*. Chicago: University of Chicago Press, 1988. Print.
Kerrane, Kevin. "Making Facts Dance." *The Art of Fact: A Historical Anthology of Literary Journalism*, edited by Kevin Kerrane and Ben Yagoda. New York: Touchstone/Simon & Schuster, 1998. 17–20. *Google Books*. Web. 13 Jan. 2016.
Kidd, Kenneth. *Making American Boys: Boyology and the Feral Tale*. Minneapolis: U of Minnesota P, 2004. Print.
Koupal, Nancy Tystad. "Introduction." *Our Landlady*, by L. Frank Baum, edited by Nancy Tystad Koupal. Lincoln: U of Nebraska P, 1996. 1–20. Print.

Kroeger, Brooke. *Nellie Bly: Daredevil, Reporter, Feminist*. New York: Times Books/Random House, 1994. Print.

Krulwich, Sara. "*Newsies* the Musical." *New York Times* 15 Nov. 2011. Photograph. Web. 20 July 2014.

London *Daily Mail* clipping, Feb.1897. Box 4. Folder 1897 n.d. Richard Harding Davis Collection (#6109). Albert and Shirley Small Special Collections Library. University of Virginia. Charlottesville, VA. 10 Dec. 2014.

London *Daily Mail* clipping, March 26, 1897. Box 4. Folder 1897 Jan.–Dec. Richard Harding Davis Collection (#6109). Albert and Shirley Small Special Collections Library. University of Virginia, Charlottesville. 11 Dec. 2014.

Lee, James Melvin. *History of American Journalism*. Garden City, NY: Garden City Publishing, 1923. Print.

Lewis, Sean. "Bud Billiken Parade Marches Down South Side." *WGNtv.com*. 9 Aug. 2014. Web. 4 March 2015.

Liddle, Dallas. *The Dynamics of Genre: Journalism and the Practice of Literature in Mid-Victorian Britain*. Charlottesville: U of Virginia P, 2009. Print.

Lutes, Jean Marie. *Front-Page Girls: Women Journalists in American Culture and Fiction, 1880–1930*. Ithaca, NY: Cornell UP, 2006. Print.

MacLeod, Anne Scott. *American Childhood: Essays on Children's Literature of the Nineteenth and Twentieth Centuries*. Athens, GA: U of Georgia P, 1994. Print.

Martin, Michelle. "African American." *Keywords for Children's Literature*, edited by Philip Nel and Lissa Paul. New York: NYU Press, 2011. 9–13. Print.

———. *Brown Gold: Milestones of African-American Children's Picture Books, 1845–2002*. New York: Routledge, 2004. Print.

McClary, Odessa. "Growing Up with the Defender." *Chicago Defender* 5 May 1975: 56. *ProQuest Historical Newspapers*. Web. 21 March 2015.

McKeon, Michael. "Theory and Practice in Historical Method." *Rethinking Historicism from Shakespeare to Milton*, edited by Ann Baynes Coiro and Thomas Fulton. Cambridge, UK: Cambridge UP, 2012. 40–64. Print.

McNair, Jonda C. "A Comparative Analysis of *The Brownies' Book* and Contemporary African American Children's Literature Written by Patricia C. McKissack." *Embracing, Evaluating, and Examining American Children's and Young Adult Literature*, edited by Wanda M. Brooks and Jonda C. McNair. Lanham, MD: Scarecrow Press, 2008. 2–29. Print.

Mercier, Cathryn M. "Realism." *Keywords for Children's Literature*, edited by

Philip Nel and Lissa Paul. New York: New York University Press, 2011. 198–201. Print.
Mintz, Steven. *Huck's Raft: A History of American Childhood.* Cambridge, MA: Harvard UP, 2004. Print.
Mitchell, Sally. *The New Girl: Girls' Culture in England 1880–1915.* New York: Columbia University Press, 1995. Print.
Montrose, Louis Adrian. "Renaissance Literary Studies and the Subject of History." *English Literary Renaissance* 16 (1986): 5–12. *JSTOR.* Web. 24 Jan. 2013.
Moon Michael. "'The Gentle Boy from the Dangerous Classes': Pederasty, Domesticity, and Capitalism in Horatio Alger." *Ragged Dick; or, Street Life in New York with Boot Blacks.* By Horatio Alger, edited by Hildegard Hoeller. Norton Critical Edition. New York: Norton, 2008. 209–33. Print.
Morris, Gouverneur. "R. H. D." *R. H. D.: Appreciations of Richard Harding Davis.* New York. Charles Scribner's Sons, 1917. 1–22. Print.
Moses, Montrose J. "Convalescent 'Children's Literature.'" *North American Review* Mar. 1925: 528. *American Periodicals.* Web. 28 Aug. 2014.
Mott, Frank Luther. *American Journalism: A History of Newspapers in the United States through 250 Years, 1690 to 1940.* New York: Macmillan, 1941. Print.
———. *Golden Multitudes: The Story of Best Sellers in the United States.* New York: Macmillan, 1947. Print.
Murray, Gail Schmunk. *American Children's Literature and the Construction of Childhood.* New York: Twayne, 1998. Print.
Myers, Walter Dean. "Where Are the People of Color in Children's Books?" *NewYorkTimes.com* 15 March 2014. Web. 18 April 2015.
Myrdal, Gunnar. *An American Dilemma: The Negro Problem and Modern Democracy.* 1944. New York: Harper & Row, 1962. Print.
Nackenoff, Carol. *The Fictional Republic: Horatio Alger and American Political Discourse.* New York: Oxford UP, 1994. Print.
Nasaw, David. *Children of the City: At Work and at Play.* New York: Oxford UP, 1985. Print.
"Nellie Bly Park." *New York City Department of Parks and Recreation.* The City of New York. 2 Nov. 2014.
Nelson, Claudia. "Girls' Fiction." *Girlhood in America: An Encyclopedia.* Santa Barbara, CA: ABC-CLIO, 2001. 327–33. Print.
"A New Literary Light. Sketch of the Rise of Richard Harding Davis." *Jackson Daily Citizen* (Jackson, MI) 31 Jan. 1891: 5. *America's Historical Newspapers.* Web. 15 Oct. 2014.

New York *World* 26 July 1896. New York Public Library Microforms Reading Room. 31 Oct. 2015.

"Other 3–No Title." *Chicago Defender* 4 Oct. 1975: 2. *ProQuest Historical Newspapers*. Web. 30 Nov. 2016.

"Oral History with Eddie Maston." 2002. Transcript. Center for Oral History and Cultural Heritage. University of Southern Mississippi Digital Collection. Web. 27 March 2015.

"Oral History with Mr. R. Jess Brown, Lawyer, Jackson, Mississippi." 1972. Transcript. Center for Oral History and Cultural Heritage. University of Southern Mississippi Digital Collection. Web. 27 March 2015.

"Oral History with Reverend Harry Charles Tartt." 2002. Transcript. Center for Oral History and Cultural Heritage. University of Southern Mississippi Digital Collection. Web. 27 March 2015.

Ottley, Roi. *The Lonely Warrior: The Life and Times of Robert S. Abbott*. Chicago: Henry Regnery, 1955. Print.

Outcault, Richard Felton. *R. F. Outcault's The Yellow Kid: A Centennial Celebration of the Kid Who Started the Comics*. Northampton, MA: Kitchen Sink Press, 1995. Print.

Paul, Lissa. "The Feminist Writer as Heroine in *Harriet the Spy*." *The Lion and the Unicorn* 13:1 (1989): 67–73. *Project Muse*. Web. 2 June 2013.

Pettegree, Andrew. *The Invention of News: How the World Came to Know About Itself*. New Haven, CT: Yale University Press, 2014. Print.

Pricola, Jennifer. "*The Brownies' Book*: Appropriating Change Through *The Brownies' Book*." University of Virginia, Spring 2003, xroads.virginia.edu/~ma03/pricola/brownies/essay9.html. 30 Jan. 2017.

Pugh, Tison. "There Lived in the Land of Oz Two Queerly Made Men: Queer Utopianism and Antisocial Eroticism in L. Frank Baum's Oz Series." *Marvels & Tales* 22:2 (2008): 217–39. Web. *Project Muse*. 4 Jan. 2014.

Pulitzer, Joseph. "The College of Journalism." *The North American Review* 178.570 (1904): 641–80. *JSTOR*. Web. 22 Nov. 2013.

Pullman, John D. *History of Education in America*. 3rd ed. Columbus, OH: Merrill Publishing, 1982. Print.

"Ragged Newsboys of New York." *New Hampshire Statesman*. 24 July 1852: Issue 1626, col. F. *19th Century U.S. Newspapers*. Web. 11 Oct. 2012.

Rahn, Suzanne. "Introduction." *L Frank Baum's World of Oz: A Classic Series at 100*, edited by Suzanne Rahn. Lanham, MD: Children's Literature Assoc. and Scarecrow Press, 2003. Print. ix–xxxv.

"Review 1—No Title." *Christian Union* 7 Aug. 1890: 183. *American Periodicals.* Web. 26 Aug. 2014.

Reynolds, Kim. *Children's Literature: A Very Short Introduction.* New York: Oxford UP, 2011. Print.

Rich, Motoko. "School Data Finds Pattern of Inequality Along Racial Lines." *NewYorkTimes.com* 21 March 2014. Web. 8 June 2014.

Rogers, Katharine. *L Frank Baum: Creator of Oz.* Cambridge, MA: Da Capo–Perseus Books, 2003. Print.

Roggenkamp, Karen. *Narrating the News: New Journalism and Literary Genre in the Late Nineteenth Century.* Kent, OH: Kent State UP, 2005. Print.

Roosevelt, Theodore. "Davis and the Rough Riders." *R. H. D.: Appreciations of Richard Harding Davis.* New York. Charles Scribner's Sons, 1917. 53–56. Print.

Rose, Jacqueline. *The Case of Peter Pan: or, The Impossibility of Children's Fiction.* London: Macmillan, 1984.

Rossiter, William S. "Printing and Publishing." *Census Reports, Twelfth Census of the United States.* Washington, DC: Government Printing Office, 1902. *Google Books.* Web. 17 Oct. 2015.

"Round the World with Nellie Bly." *The World* 26 Jan. 1890. Library of Congress. Web. 17 Jan. 2015.

Rudd, David. "Theorizing and Theories: How Does Children's Literature Exist?" *Understanding Children's Literature*, edited by Peter Hunt. New York: Routledge, 1999. 15–29. Print.

Sachsman, David W., and David W. Bulla. "Introduction." *Sensationalism: Murder, Mayhem, Mudslinging, Scandals, and Disasters in 19th Century Reporting*, edited by David W. Sachsman and David W. Bulla. New Brunswick, NJ: Transaction Publishers, 2013. xvii–xxxiv. Print.

Sanchez-Eppler, Karen. *Dependent States: The Child's Part in Nineteenth-Century American Culture.* Chicago: U of Chicago P, 2005. Print.

Scharnhorst, Gary. "Demythologizing Alger." *Ragged Dick; or, Street Life in New York with Boot Blacks.* By Horatio Alger, edited by Hildegard Hoeller. Norton Critical Edition. New York: Norton, 2008. 182–98. Print.

———. "'He Is Amusing but Not Inherently a Gentleman': The Vexed Relations of Kate Field and Samuel Clemens." *Legacy* 18:2 (2001): 193–204. Web. 12 Nov. 2014.

Scharnhorst, Gary, and Jack Bales. *The Lost Life of Horatio Alger, Jr.* Bloomington: Indiana UP, 1985. Print.

Schudson, Michael. *Discovering the News: A Social History of American Newspapers*. New York: Basic Books/Perseus Books, 1978. Print.

———. "Why News Is the Way It Is." *Raritan* 2:3 (1983): 109–25. Print.

Seelye, John D. *War Games: Richard Harding Davis and the New Imperialism*. Amherst: U of Massachusetts P, 2003. Print.

"Service with a Smile." *The Tacoma Times* 16 Jan. 1917: 2. *Chronicling America*. Library of Congress. Web. 20 Jan. 2015.

Setoodeh, Ramin. "The Cult of *Newsies*." *The Daily Beast*, 10 Oct. 2011. Web. 7 June 2014.

Shapiro, Anne Dhu. "Action Music in American Pantomime and Melodrama, 1730–913." *American Music* 2:4 (1984): 49–72. *JSTOR*. Web. 29 Sept. 2014.

Shelden, Michael. *Mark Twain: Man in White: The Grand Adventures of His Final Years*. New York: Random House, 2010. Print.

Smith, Katharine Capshaw. *Children's Literature of the Harlem Renaissance*. Bloomington: Indiana UP, 2004. Print.

Sontag, Susan. *Susan Sontag: Essays of the 1960s and 70s*, edited by David Rieff. New York: Library of America–Penguin, 2013.

Stahl, J. D. "Satire and the Evolution of Perspective in Children's Literature: Mark Twain, E. B. White, and Louise Fitzhugh." *Children's Literature Association Quarterly* 15:3 (1990): 119–22. *Project Muse*. Web. 2 June 2013.

Stephens, Mitchell. *A History of News: From the Drum to the Satellite*. New York: Viking–Penguin, 1988. Print.

"Story of Nellie Bly An Authentic Biography of the Little Globe-Gridler." *Grand Forks Daily Herald* (*Daily Herald*; Grand Forks, ND. Reprinted from the New York *World*) 24 Feb. 1890: 3. *America's Historical Newspapers*. Web. 1 Nov. 2014.

Stowe, Gene. *Inherit the Land: Jim Crow Meets Miss Maggie's Will*. Jackson: UP of Mississippi, 2006. *Google Books*. Web. 18 April 2015.

Tarkington, Booth. Untitled. *R. H. D.: Appreciations of Richard Harding Davis*. New York. Charles Scribner's Sons, 1917. 23–28. Print.

"Three Vancouver Girls Newspaper's Sole Staff." *Oregonian* (*Morning Oregonian*; Portland, Oregon). 18 Feb. 1912: 14. *America's Historical Newspapers*. Web. 26 Oct. 2014.

Twain, Mark. *A Connecticut Yankee in King Arthur's Court*. 1889. New York: Penguin, 1986. Print.

Undated New York *World* clipping, circa 1895. "Three Gringoes at Home" by Arthur Brisbane. Box 3. Folder 1895 April–n.d. Richard Harding Davis. Collection (#6109). Albert and Shirley Small Special Collections Library. University of Virginia. Charlottesville, VA. 10 Dec. 2014.

Vaughn-Robertson, Courtney, and Brenda Hill. "*The Brownies' Book* and Ebony Jr.!: Literature as a Mirror of the Afro-American Experience." *Journal of Negro Education* 58:4 (1989): 494–510. Web. 12 June 2014.

Weikle-Mills, Courtney. *Imaginary Citizens: Child Readers and the Limits of American Independence 1640–1868.* Baltimore: Johns Hopkins UP, 2013. Print.

White, Hayden. "The Value of Narrativity in the Representation of Reality." *On Narrative*, edited by W. J. T. Mitchell. Chicago: U of Chicago P, 1980. 1–23. Print.

Wiebe, Robert H. *The Search for Order 1877–1920.* New York: Hill and Wang, 1967. Print.

Winfield, Betty Houchin, and Janice Hume. *The Continuous Past: Historical Referents in Nineteenth-Century American Journalism.* Columbia, SC: Association for Education in Journalism and Mass Communication, 2007. Print.

Wolf, Virginia L. "Readers of *Alice*: My Children, Meg Murray, and Harriet M. Welsch." *Children's Literature Association Quarterly* 13:3 (1988): 135–37. JSTOR. Web. 6 June 2013.

Wolfe, Tom. "From *The Electric Kool-Aid Acid Test*." *The New Journalism*, edited by Tom Wolfe and E. W. Johnson. New York: Harper and Row, 1973. Print. 204–18.

———. "The Kandy-Kolored Tangerine-Flake Streamline Baby." *The Kandy-Kolored Tangerine-Flake Streamline Baby*. New York: Farrar, Straus, and Giroux. 76–106. Print.

———. "The New Journalism." *The New Journalism,* edited by Tom Wolfe and E. W. Johnson. New York: Harper and Row, 1973. Print. 3–23.

"Women and the Newspapers." *Topeka Weekly Capital* (*Kansas Weekly Capital and Farm Journal*) 3 Nov. 1892: Supplement 13. *America's Historical Newspapers*. Web. 26 Oct. 2014.

Young, Kevin. *Bunk: The Rise of Hoaxes, Humbug, Plagiarists, Phonies, Post-Facts, and Fake News.* Minneapolis: Graywolf Press, 2017.

Zelizer, Barbie. "When Facts, Truth and Reality are God-terms: On Journalism's Uneasy Place in Cultural Studies." *Communication and Critical/Cultural Studies* 1 (2004): 100–19. Sage. Web. 22 Feb. 2014.

Zipes, Jack, Lissa Paul, Lynne Vallone, Peter Hunt, and Gillian Avery. "Preface." *The Norton Anthology of Children's Literature*, edited by Jack Zipes, Lissa Paul, Lynne Vallone, Peter Hunt, and Gillian Avery. New York: Norton, 2005. Print. xxv–xxxv

INDEX

Abbott, Robert, 74–75, 112
Alcott, Louisa May, xviii, 43
Aldrich, Thomas Bailey, 23
Alger, Horatio Jr.
   Ben Bruce, 14–16
   Ben the Luggage Boy, 12
   Dan, thea Detective, 14
   The Errand Boy, 12
   Luke Walton, 14
   Ragged Dick, 5–6, 11
   myth-making of, 6
   and newsboys, 10
   relationship with newspapers, 10–11
   Rough and Ready, 3, 11, 12–13
   The Telegraph Boy, 12
Alice in Wonderland. *See* Carroll, Lewis
American Revolution, xxvi, 103
The Atlantic, xxviii, xxxi, 15, 106
Aunt Jane's Nieces. *See* Dyne, Edith Van

Baum, L. Frank
   The Aberdeen Saturday Pioneer, 6, 53, 56
   The Art of Decorating Dry Good Windows, 47–48
   Aunt Jane's Nieces, 51
   Aunt Jane's Nieces on Vacation, 45, 46, 58–61, 64–68
   Dyne, Edith Van, 43–45, 46, 50, 68
   The Wizard of Oz, xxxv, 41–42, 48, 50–53, 58, 60, 61, 63, 68
   See also Dyne, Edith Van
Bly, Nellie, xxix, 41, 42, 49, 54–56, 110
Brecht, Bertolt, xxxiii
The Brownies' Book, 73–74, 82, 111, 112

Carroll, Lewis, 23, 104
Chicago Defender, 70–71, 73, 74–76, 112. *See also* Chicago Defender Junior
Chicago Defender Junior, xxvi, xxv
   Billikin Parade, 70–71, 86
   Bud Billikin, 72, 76–79
   geographic diversity of club members, 80–81
   poetry, 82–84
   promotion and readership of, 78, 84–86
   See also *Chicago Defender*
Children's literature, study of, xxxii–xxxiv
   African American children's literature, 72–74
   agency of children in, xxxiii–xxxiv
   boy books, 23–24
   girl series fiction, 43–44
   Golden Age of, xviii, xxi, xxxii–xxxiiv, 5, 22, 23, 47, 90, 91, 94, 104
Civil War (American), xv, xvii, xxxi, xxxiv, 5, 35, 47
The Crisis, 73, 74

Davis, Rebecca, 17, 25
   Life in the Iron-Mills, xxx, 21
Davis, Richard Harding
   celebrity and popularity of, 20–21
   Cuba and the Spanish-American War, 36–38
   early life, 25
   foreign correspondence, 17–18
   "Gallegher," xxxv, 20, 25–33, 39, 108

Davis, Richard Harding (*cont'd*)
   Gallegher and Other Stories, 17
   "The Reporter Who Made Himself King," xxxv, 18, 20, 33–39
   Soldiers of Fortune, 20
   Stories for Boys, 33, 108
   writing career, 25
Du Bois, W.E.B, 73, 74
Dunbar, Paul Laurence, 82–84
Dyne, Edith Van, 43–45, 46, 50, 68
   Aunt Jane's Nieces, 51
   Aunt Jane's Nieces on Vacation, 45, 46, 58–61, 64–68
   See also Baum, L. Frank

Elizabeth Cochran. *See* Bly, Nellie
Emerson, Ralph Waldo, 26, 108
epic theater, xxxiv

Field, Kate, 54
Fitzhugh, Louise. See *Harriet the Spy*

Gage, Matilda, 51–53, 56, 57
"Gallegher." *See under* Davis, Richard Harding
Gibson, Charles Dana, 21

Harper's, xxviii, 17, 20, 31, 106, 112
Harriet the Spy, xxxvi, 90
   and journalism, 98–100
   reception of, 92–93
Hawthorne, Nathaniel, xxx
Hearst, William Randolph, xxiv, xxvii, 37, 48, 75, 103, 105, 108, 109, 110. See also *The New York Journal*
Hogan's Alley, xiii–xv, xviii, xxii–xxiv, xxv, xxvi, 101. *See also* Yellow Kid
Howells, William Dean, 15
   The Rise of Silas Lapham, xxi
   Huckleberry Finn. *See* Twain, Mark

journalism
   African American journalism, 74–76, 111 (see also *Chicago Defender*)
   brief American history of, xxvi–xxix
   new journalism (late nineteenth century), 37–39, 55, 114
   New Journalism (twentieth century), 89–92, 94–101, 114
   newspaper growth in America, 9–10
   women working in, 53–58, 62–63, 110, 111
   yellow journalism, xxii–xxiii, xxiv, xxix, 37, 43, 103, 108, 109

Life in the Iron-Mills. *See* Davis, Rebecca
Little Women. *See* Alcott, Louisa May

McClure's Magazine, xxiv, xxix, 104
Motley, Willard, 78. *See also* Chicago Defender Junior
muckraking, xxix, 114

New Journalism. *See under* journalism
new realism, 93
newsboys
   and cultural performance, 13–16
   historical accounts of, 7–8
   of the popular imagination, 5–7
   See also Alger, Horatio, Jr., *Newsies*
Newsboys Lodging House, 10
Newsies (musical), 1–2, 16, 105
New York Journal, xxiv, 37, 105, 109

Oliver Optic (book series), xviii
"Our Landlady" (newspaper column), 56. *See also*, Baum, L. Frank

Pulitzer, Joseph, xiii, xv, xxiv, xxvii, xxviii, 27, 41, 46, 48, 55, 105, 108, 109, 110, 111. See also *The World*

realism (American), xxx–xxxii, 15, 21, 47, 93, 95
"The Reporter Who Made Himself King." *See under* Davis, Richard Harding
The Rise of Silas Lapham. See under Howells, William Dean
Romanticism (American), xxx

Sontag, Susan, xx
Spanish-American War, 20, 107
  Cuba, 36–38
St. Nicholas, 23, 111

Tom Sawyer. See under Twain, Mark
Twain, Mark, xxxi, 22–23, 47, 113
  A Connecticut Yankee in King Arthur's Court, 104
  Huckleberry Finn, 23, 24
  Tom Sawyer, xvii, 23, 24

Uncle Tom's Cabin, xxx, xxxii

The Wizard of Oz. See under Baum, L. Frank
Wolfe, Tom, xxxvi
  The Electric Kool-Aid Acid Test, 96, 114
  "Kandy-Kolored Tangerine-Flake Streamline Baby," 89–90, 95
  and New Journalism, 89–90, 94–95, 114
  The New Journalism, 94
The World, xiii–xv, xxii–xxv, xxviii, 21, 39, 41, 42, 48, 49, 54, 105, 110, 111. *See also* Pulitzer, Joseph

yellow journalism. *See under* journalism
Yellow Kid, xiii, xxii–xxvi, 101, 103, 109–110

www.ingramcontent.com/pod-product-compliance
Lightning Source LLC
Chambersburg PA
CBHW020935230426
43666CB00008B/1690